Matt,

I'M RIVELINO

A LIFE OF TWO HALVES
****

Andy Rivers

This'll be worth Millions
When I'm Dead .... ☺

Byker Books

Cheers

Published by:-

Byker Books
Banbury
Oxon
OX16 0DJ

www.bykerbooks.co.uk

2009

ISBN 978-0-9560788-2-7

Typeset by Byker Books, Banbury

Printed in Great Britain by Lightning Source, Milton Keynes

To all the friends I made along the way...

I'm Rivelino - A Life of Two Halves

Foreword by Lee Clark

I was born on Tyneside in the Seventies and grew up surrounded by football and Newcastle United in particular. As you know I played for 'The Toon' and was proud to do so - always will be - and I felt I had a genuine bond with the supporters, being one of them myself. As the saying goes' If I wasn't on the pitch wearing black and white I'd have been on the terraces wearing it' and with that in mind I can relate to the stories in this book. Andy Rivers has told an entertaining tale about growing up and following 'your' team through thick and thin - I think most football fans will read this and think he could just as easily have written about their team.

I'm sure you'll enjoy it - whichever team you support.

Best Wishes

Lee Clark

I'm Rivelino - A Life of Two Halves

Punditry Bollocks

Roberto Rivelino made his name worldwide with his vicious cannon-like free-kicks, long range shooting and dribbling skills. One particularly famous move of his, called the elastic dribble, is still imitated today. He scored many times with this move often leaving his opponents open-mouthed and wrong footed in his wake.

He was twenty four when he won the Mexico world cup in 1970. That Brazilian team is regarded by many as the best ever and it displayed some of the finest football ever seen with Rivelino as one of the best players. He scored three great goals including a trademark thunderous free-kick against Czechoslovakia in their first match.

In his prime Rivelino was one of the greatest offensive midfielders in the world and, in a show of loyalty that most modern day players couldn't begin to understand, spent most of his career at Corinthians. The fans appreciated this and nicknamed him Reizinho do Parque (King of the Park). He retired in 1981 and is today a respected TV pundit in Brazil.

Andy 'Rivelino' Rivers, spent most of his football career at centre half for deeply average school teams, a cartilage injury when he was fourteen started the decline in his already mediocre record to the point where, at the age of twenty one and with two operations behind him, he finished his playing days at the heart of Westholme Farm Social Club's defence. The North Tyneside league never really knew what it had missed.

So there you have it, two men with spookily similar careers, the only difference being that one was a Brazilian international who was idolised by millions of people, played at the highest level and won the highest honour possible in his chosen career and the other didn't.

In all other respects they could have been twins...

6

FIRST HALF

SECOND HALF

.......STILL PLAYING.......

First Half

Welcome to the North

Flowers and Football Tops

I buried one of my best mates on Christmas Eve 2004, Col was thirty five years old and like me had never seen his club, Newcastle United, win a thing.

Driving up from my self- imposed exile in deepest, darkest Oxfordshire for his funeral two days before Christmas was a sombre affair. I was travelling on my own and had promised my wife I'd be back early on Christmas Day which gave me nearly five hours in holiday traffic with just my thoughts, memories and that irritating twat Chris Moyles for company.

Having a funeral on Christmas Eve appears to have some kind of celestial symmetry to it - you know, the birth of the main man, the end of the year and all that - it should make you think about stuff on a higher plane. But when you're seeing off one of your pals all you can think about then is drinking to his memory and saying goodbye. Particularly when that mate has shuffled off his mortal coil at such a young age with a lot of unfulfilled ambitions and dreams.

So I was in reflective mood as I nosed the car up the M1 and the smell of Yorkshire hit me. The stench of what seemed like cow shit and cabbage transporting me back to a far off land where it was always sunny, there was always beer to drink and me and Col always managed to have a good time no matter how many we'd lost by that day.

Glancing up I caught sight of myself in the rearview mirror and noticed a small smile on my face - that bastard had sneaked in when I wasn't looking.

Then I saw the sign indicating the Barnsley turnoff and I burst out laughing - my finest moment as the designated match driver. I'd managed to buckle the wheel of my employers sandwich van and get lost on the way home ... oh and we got beat...and it had been on the telly anyway. Col gave me stick all the way back from that one and never let me live it down - but the thing he used to say to me most, particularly on that day, stuck with me all the way back home for his send off.

'We should write a book Rivs...'

The funeral itself was by necessity a sad occasion, he was a relatively young man with a family and I didn't feel much like talking after but went for a pint with the rest of the lads anyway. It was about halfway through the afternoon and I was in a pub I didn't like much, just reminiscing about Col when it struck me that this was it. I had one pop at this life and I was already half way through it. As well as my own personal underachievement Newcastle hadn't done a great deal either during my lifetime and worse still it didn't look fucking likely from where I was standing. I stopped drinking after that as I wanted to get home for Christmas and I'd suddenly realised I had a lot to do.

I got up at about two in the morning on Christmas Day and got the car and my stuff ready for the long drive home. Waving goodbye to me mam I pondered the journey ahead - it was going to be a long one.

But then it already had been.

<u>Awakenings</u>

'I'm Pele.'

'Nah man I'm Pele.'

'Well I'm Kevin Keegan then.'

'Who are you Simon?'

'Me, I'm Kenny Dalglish.'

'Bastard, I wish I'd thought of that.'

'You swore, I'm telling Miss.'

That was Hardcastle, snivelling little grass. He was shite at football and claimed he didn't like it. Welbeck Road Juniors in the Seventies was no place for a lad who didn't like football and he had to play with the lasses most days.

'Who can I be then?' I whinged as six year olds did at dinnertime when all the good players were already taken.

'You Andy. You can be Rivelino.'

'Rivelino?'

'Aye man, he scored that free kick in the world cup. Me dad said he was deed good.'

'HA HA - you're called Rivers and Simon said you could be Rivelino. That means you're Riverslino. Ha Ha.'

'Piss off man Hardcastle.' Deka smacked him in the face and he ran off crying, looking for a teacher. Deka was my mate, which was good because he was massive...well for a six year old anyway.

'Reet then.' I said, happy at being thought worthy of a Brazilian nickname and knowing in my heart it was because all the lads compared my skills to the South American trickster's and not because my surname was vaguely similar to a little known ex-international.

'We're kicking towards the dinner huts and I'm Rivelino.'

Aye, them were the days. That's my very first football memory, probably Hardcastle's first taste of football violence as well. However, my first proper experience of professional football was in the '76 season, we hadn't long moved to Byker from Wallsend and Uncle Charlie took me to the match with him. I can vaguely remember us playing Arsenal, me and some other kid hanging about outside a pub for a while and then sitting on a barrier bored and it being absolute shite. Obviously that was me sold and set for a lifetime of misery, cheers Charlie.

At that age football consisted of watching 'Shoot' on a Sunday afternoon, for those of you who don't know this was a regional highlights programme that operated a strict rotational policy no matter which division your team was in. In practice this usually involved you sitting through an hour of Carlisle United (fucking Carlisle isn't even in the North East) versus Darlington and then at the end you got two minutes of Newcastle being twatted four nowt off some Cockney team. I once sat in and watched it all the way through while my mates played in the street outside, purely to witness the mighty Peter Withe score in a three one defeat to Brighton. In the interests of balance I have to point out that obviously as well as Shoot you also had Match of the Day on BBC One, but if you didn't support or want to watch Liverpool then this was utterly pointless, a bit similar to supporting Sunderland really, enough said.

Anyway, at the tender age of six there was no way I'd be going to the match on a regular basis and there was no way Uncle Charlie wanted to interrupt his pre match drinking to take the nephew along so Shoot was the closest I got. The real football action at that age was in the street where as inventive, future bouncers, entrepreneurs, plumbers, butchers and drug dealing layabouts we created games that would keep us occupied for hours on end. The names trip off the tongue even now, Gates, Three Pots In, Headers and Volleys, Spot and of course Kerbs. You can stick your playstations, social networking internet sites and bedrooms full of DVD players up your arse, proper kids played these games, usually in packs of twenty or so and always with some blood and tears mixed into the equation.

During the epochal (well it was for me anyway) season when I saw my first live game and fell in love with the club that was to be my life for the rest of my life, we achieved something that has happened only twice since - we got to a cup final. Granted it was only the league cup and not the sexy FA version but we were there. We'd fucked up badly in the '74 cup final but I'd been too young to understand that. Now though at the age of six I was old enough to know what was going on. Actually, in this city, where Grannies who've never been to the match can tell you who's shit and who's not trying and even people who don't like football can tell you why we never win anything, I was probably old enough to have an actual opinion.

All I can remember of the game was that we lost and an alleged Geordie (Dennis Tueart - wanker) had scored the winner past us with an overhead kick. It didn't matter that we'd had a weakened team or that we had laid the ghost of the spineless FA cup final team from two years previous, we'd still lost. Now obviously as a six year old who knew that we'd been in a final not that long ago this wasn't the end of the world as obviously we'd be there again quite soon wouldn't we? All these adults that filled my house drinking Party Sevens and singing Blaydon Races were always telling me how we were the best team in the world so it stood to reason that we'd win it next year. Oh the innocence of youth.

Me and the lads were soon out in the street playing Cup Finals, the misery of losing at Wembley immediately forgotten, well unless you claimed to be Dennis Tueart, you soon got a clout if that was the case. Me, I was still Rivelino; Brazil had never beaten Newcastle in a cup final so that was alright.

Fast forward six years and Newcastle's fortunes had plummeted, the team's decline mirroring that of the city as the unemployment lines grew longer and belts got tighter. I had moved on to comprehensive education and had made new friends, my world consisting of playing schools football and keeping an eye out for the results of my, now second division, team.

The club itself seemed punch drunk, lurching from crisis to crisis (nowt changes eh) and ironically, as the country seemed full of them at that time, we really needed a striker. We'd been through a succession of nonentities, has beens and never will be's in search of a player to capture the imagination of an area in despair. Then in the August of '82 in the most audacious coup ever, my team, Newcastle United of the second division, signed the former England captain Kevin Keegan from Southampton and the place went mental. Records were released, thousands of words written in the press and many, many pints were sunk, but most importantly the whole city started believing in itself and it's footballing representative again.

For the first match of that season we were up against Queens Park Rangers, they were managed by the highly rated and relatively young Terry Venables and were expected to do good things that year. The match, so far as I can tell, was magic. The place was buzzing and the cameras had found their way to St. James Park once again (someone probably conned them that Liverpool were there.).

Where was I? I was in the house listening to the Radio because a mate's dad who had promised to take my eleven year old self to the match had stayed in the boozer leaving me with no option but to listen to the worlds shitest commentator.

In a moment of pure theatre, the kind of story you couldn't make up cos it would be too corny, Keegan scored the only goal of the game. I've watched it that many times since on video that I can describe it without thinking.

Craggs at right back knocked it up the wing, Keegan flicked it on, Varadi headed it into space for him to run onto and, as the crowd went into overdrive, the great man kept his cool and slotted it under Hucker the QPR keeper at the Gallowgate End. He was mobbed by dozens after that goal and probably learnt what Newcastle was all about in the minute it took him to break free.

We were a city that had suffered badly in the recession, probably more than most, and were desperate to hold our heads high again - the signing of Keegan allowed us that privilege and, more than that, the man himself, with his positive outlook and honest approach, gave us hope that things would get better.

He was exactly what we needed and lived up to all of our expectations...more than once.

DOG EAT DOG

The Eighties

Manchester City (h) 83-84

Have you ever delivered them free papers? You know the ones - they all carry adverts for stuff you'll never ever buy and you just tend to use them for putting at the bottom of your budgies cage and that. Well around about this time I was delivering them - a penny a paper I got and that was considered good money amongst the teenage delivery lads on our estate, in fact it was like promotion getting off the local evening rag round and getting onto the freebies. So instead of dragging myself around the doors every night and battling guard dogs through letterboxes I only had to do it once a week but, as I've already said, I only got a penny a paper so in order to get my match money I had to take on a round that entailed five hundred of these bastards.

Can you imagine lifting a bag with five hundred papers in it? Add in the leaflets that these sadists always stuck in and you're talking some weight there. I was only thirteen and I had a right arm like Fatima Whitbread (that might not have been the papers mind) but when you're playing Man City on the Saturday it was worth every minute of trudging round the estate in the rain delivering papers that no-one ever read. This was a top of the table clash as our promotion season gathered full momentum, the outlandish and still, frankly fucking astonishing, capture of Kevin Keegan the year previous had fired the imagination of all of us (doesn't take much like)and the whole Geordie Nation was getting behind the team as we marched on to our rightful home in Division One.

And what a team it was - well actually, as a team we weren't that good at all but any club that can play Waddle, Beardsley and Keegan up front and in their prime will always have a chance. We were playing some cracking stuff. Genuine one touch, pass and move, triangular football that thrilled the purists, not that there were many of them in the toon in those days, which resulted in loads of goals and, most importantly, won us games.

This match was seen as a pointer to who would be filling the top positions come May and as such we all approached the ground with a little bit of trepidation. But, as was always the case back then, (maybe not so much now) no cowardice was displayed in the face of the enemy and St. James was a cauldron of boiling Geordie pride as we sang our defiance and our support with one voice. After eight minutes we were one up, the mighty Peter Beardsley opening both his account and the floodgates. Just before half-time Wor Kev netted to put us two up and to make the half time Bovril (I was only thirteen remember - I didn't start drinking for another year) taste all the sweeter, or less like shite, depending on your point of view.

After the break we took the piss and here's an example of just how much. Who remembers Wes Saunders? Just me? Thought so. He was a local lad who was lucky enough to play in our defence when he wasn't really that good, his biggest claim to fame was being caught 'allegedly' shop lifting in the city centre a la Winona Ryder. Anyway, even he had a shot cleared off the line - that's how much we were on top.

The third goal had to come and it did in the sixtieth minute, Waddle met Beardsley's cross and the highly rated (and on the day bloody overworked) Alec Williams in the City goal parried it only for the ever alert Mr Beardsley to lash it home. Wor Peter completed his hatrick soon after, racing through the defence to poke it home whilst we celebrated wildly on the terraces (remember them?) and then, near the end, Waddle completed the rout, he took a McDermott pass and lashed a low twenty yarder past Williams to make it five. Beardsley said afterwards that he'd just chased everything in pursuit of his third goal as Arthur Cox, the manager, had substituted Waddle a few weeks previously because 'he hadn't looked hungry enough for his hatrick.' Walking home after the match, bathed in the warm afterglow of an afternoon when everything had gone right I knew that this was the season, we were going up.

Leicester (a) 84-85

I'd been going regularly to home matches by now and was itching to make the long trip out of Newcastle to somewhere else in this great country of ours (as you know, every trip from the toon is a long one). The only things stopping me from actually doing it were cash and me mam but an opportunity soon presented itself. The local water board head office and treatment works had its own social club on our estate (sounds boring I know but bear with me) and a couple of lads and myself had discovered one afternoon that they stacked their crates full of empties outside the back door of this club ready for collection by the draymen when they made their delivery. After a small fact finding mission at the local shop all of two hundred yards away we discovered that the shopkeeper would pay us five pence for each empty bottle we delivered to him - game on.

The six foot wall topped with broken glass was designed to keep intruders that were intent on industrial espionage or sabotage or something out of the water board premises. It was never going to stop three scrotes from the estate getting in and spiriting away the empties though, come on man, we were Byker lads after all. We'd be over that wall every night when it got dark and every Sunday Morning before opening time, never taking all of the crates though. Latif, the shopkeeper, hadn't realised what he'd let himself in for when he promised us five pence a bottle, we were robbing them left, right and centre and I soon had the money for an away trip put by, unfortunately greed kept me going back for more and the stewards who ran the club finally realised that the brewery weren't taking the bottles.

One Sunday morning, we were on top of the wall and ready to jump down when I noticed the normally locked fire door was ajar. Smelling a twenty stone rat a couple of seconds too late I hit the ground hard and immediately headed for the main gate, I wasn't a moment too soon. The fire door burst open to reveal a motley crew of moustachioed fat bastards with snooker cues in their hands and grim expressions on their faces. The other two lads soon overtook me, I may not have mentioned this before but I'm not that fast, and I could feel the lynch mob getting closer.

Now I've watched a lot of them nature programmes on the telly and I know what to do if I ever get chased by a crocodile but none of them ever told you how to go about losing a pack of fat club men. The hot, beery breath on my neck and the chubby fingers trying to grab my T-shirt collar prompted some creative thinking on my part, I've always looked older than I am and knew they wouldn't believe I was fourteen, I'd even been getting served in pubs recently. I knew I was on for a kicking.

I quickly looked over my shoulder at the chasing mob to gauge their size, one of them was closer to me than the rest, they looked like giving up having made their point but this twat was manic looking and was definitely looking forward to being the hero. Time for action, not least to stop him ripping my new T-shirt, it was a fucking Adidas Lendl man. I veered left sharply, then right, then left again to create a bit of space (see I know how to play Alan if you ever need a striker) and then made my move. I stopped dead, spun one hundred and eighty degrees and booted him hard in the nuts. He sunk to the ground clasping his plums with the confused expression you would associate with a lion who'd just been twatted by the wildebeest he was trying to eat. The rest of the pack lost interest in me after that and I skipped away to the sound of half hearted threats and abuse and decided I'd leave the crates from now on. I had the money I needed anyway, I just had to persuade me mam to let us go to Leicester.

But, in the end, even that was easy, I simply told her that a school mate's dad was going to go and he would take us along with the official supporters club, she was fine with that so it was all on. I joined the club and booked my place on the coach along with a lad from school and then applied for my ticket. This was to be our first game back in the big league, our triumphant return to Division One and I wanted to be there, there'd be no more King Kev this season but I was sure we'd be alright. We'd got Big Jack Charlton in as manager during the close season and he'd be great, a local lad who'd won the World Cup - fantastic.

I couldn't sleep for a week beforehand (mainly because I lived too close to that water board club and I could hear the bastards going past our house most nights - ho hum) but then the time came - my first away match. The begging, cajoling and whingeing sessions I'd put in on me mam over the entire close season had paid off and now we were back in Division One and I was going to be there. My abiding memory over the six weeks school holidays was of Beardsley's lob gently arcing over massive Joe Corrigan's head and I wanted more. We'd had Keegan's testimonial, the stage managed two's each draw with the mighty Liverpool, the packed crowd and the emotional farewell by helicopter but this was the real thing. The fixture list had been relatively kind for our first match back in the top division and I knew we'd win. I knew it with all the certainty a fourteen year old boy could have, just as I knew the best way to steal a Mars Bars from the local shop and how blowing in a lasses ear made her knickers fall off - piece of piss man.

This was going to be my first ever time out of Newcastle on my own and I wasn't even sure where Leicester was (actually I'm still not) but I didn't care, that's because I genuinely was going on a supporters bus and they would put us at the ground so we didn't really need to know our way around. Obviously I'd neglected to mention that my mate's dad wasn't actually coming and that it was the independent supporters club but hey, we're talking street cred at school here.

Incidentally joining the supporters club was easy, do you remember them little huts that used to be next to 'The Farmers' boozer behind Marks and Spencer? Actually, do you remember the pub? For any younger readers the Farmers was the best pre-match bar in town, loads of good music, belting atmosphere and a good, eclectic selection of veteran radgies - you can keep your plastic, sanitised, tabloid myth Quayside - I'm old school me. Anyway, I went to the supporters club shop...or hut as it should have been called, and signed up.

Some dotty old woman who should really have known better took my details and a token fee, gave me a membership card and that was me in. My mate did the same, we'd sorted the match tickets and we were ready.

On the bus we were surrounded by various looney tunes and there was loads of singing, we saw bus after bus and car after car filled with black and white on the motorway going down there, it seemed like the whole of Geordieland was heading to Leicester that day and we were lapping it up. We'd got some booze and were necking it surreptitiously in our seats, talking manicly about how we were men now and mixing with the big lads as equals. How we'd maybe 'get stuck in to some Leicester' if they dared to mess with us, then, in the next breath, contradicting ourselves with how we'd boast about this at school on Monday but we hoped our mams didn't find out. Our neighbours must have been pissing themselves at these two bum fluffed, squeaky voiced, spotty dafties - in fact I know they must have been because I do the same now whenever I see two charvas acting the big lads at the match - I usually spend the whole ninety minutes taking the piss out of them.

We got to the outskirts of Leicester and started cruising slowly through the streets in convoy towards the ground, at this point the steward on the bus made his way up the aisle informing us all to 'keep your heads down lads and try to stay as far away from the windows as possible'. We were still full of the drink at this point and laughed off this threat to our safety with flippant remarks about 'knocking the fuckers out', then we rounded a corner and saw the biggest gang of young, fit, scary looking, blokes I'd ever seen outside of a pub and I was suddenly sober and had my head down.

At the match, my arse back in my trousers and my bottle picked back up off the floor I joined in the drunken singing and chanting in the packed away end. There were estimates that day of ten thousand Geordies in Leicester and I couldn't confirm or deny it but I know it was fucking full in there. The match itself was what Sky television would now call classic Newcastle United

We went one nil up courtesy of David Mcreery, one of only two goals he scored in over two hundred and fifty appearances for the mags, they equalised, we dragged it back to 2-1 - thank you Mr. Waddle - they equalised again and we were heading for an away draw as our first result back in the top flight, no disgrace at all.

Steve 'the wall' Carney, a Wallsend lad born and bred, had other ideas though and scored his only goal ever for the toon to gain us a late three - two victory. I was ecstatic, the other nine thousand nine hundred and ninety nine Geordies were a bit pleased as well, mind you the locals weren't happy surprisingly enough and there were little kick offs outside the ground as we filed out.

We got back on the bus in happy mood, singing and chanting all the way through the streets of Leicester, a four hour drive awaited us with no booze left for comfort but we didn't care - United were back.

Ps - for those of you who started watching football around about the time Sky started broadcasting it I would like to make it clear that Manchester United do not in fact hold copyright on the term 'United' and as a Newcastle fan of many years standing I am, in fact, quite entitled to use it in reference to my team - so I fucking will. Got that? Good.

__Mackems (h) 84-85__

Last New Years day I walked into town, freezing despite my Christmas jumper, and moaned all the way there. Obviously nowt changes because in nineteen eighty five I did the very same thing only I was a bit younger, fitter and hairier.

George Orwell's prophetic year had passed and we weren't enslaved by the state, spied on or manipulated by government and corporation controlled media. Mind you he was only about twenty years out - not a bad punt at it really, nice one George.

Anyway, this match was a big one, all matches against the great unwashed are but this had a bit of significance. Our promotion twelve months earlier had seen the shock departure of manager Arthur Cox. In true Newcastle United fashion our board of directors had reneged on promises and expected him to grin and bear it, unfortunately Arthur was old school and told them to stick their job up their arse. So we lost the man who'd had the foresight and bollocks to approach the former captain of England to play for our second division team, the man who had revolutionised our style of play to the extent that we regularly scored four and five goals and the man who had, most importantly, given a struggling Northern city facing a bleak future under a southern facing Tory government back it's pride and belief.

In his place we got a true Northern man, a Geordie and a world cup winner. As I've already mentioned, while the press speculated on the various up and comers that we might attract, your Bobby Robsons (if only...), Terry Venables and Brian Cloughs (yeh right) we got....Jack Charlton.

His appointment wasn't immediately welcomed by the fans in fact, in fairness he was never accepted by the majority of them. In what is now seen as a pattern of increasing regularity employed by whichever miscreant is in the chairman's chair we had gone from a manager who espoused expansive, attractive football to a knock it long and keep it tight merchant.

From a good start we'd fallen down the league and by the time this game came around we needed a win badly.

I was in my second last year at school by now and spent most of my time getting knocked back by lasses, playing computer games (Manic Miner on the Spectrum - absolute class man) and trying to make money. My freebie paper round had been sub-contracted to my little brother, my scam with the empty bottles had been stopped dead and I needed a new source of income so I could keep going to the match - to further complicate this I looked about twenty even though I was fourteen which meant I couldn't get in for the juniors price anymore. Unfair I know but when you're from Byker you expect that anyway - you just have to get around it.

Salvation came in the form of a certain frozen food shop at the top of Shields Road, I started working late nights there on a Thursday and Friday to supplement my match day income and I was sorted, as me mam said at the time 'Son's gone to Iceland' - I'll get me coat.

Back to the game, I'd walked over Byker Bridge into town in the snow and the sleet with a sense of foreboding - not because they were any good, I just hated playing these bastards - I still do. For a full week before we play them my stomach ties itself up in knots and the thoughts swirl around my tortured head.

What if they fluke a goal?

What if they badly injure our best players?

God, what if somehow our entire team is replaced by martian robots and they conspire to cheat us and we go down? (I was reading a lot of Roy of the Rovers at the time - don't judge me.) In the event I needn't have worried - mind you we still, in true toon fashion, did our best to throw it away.

Sir Peter Beardsley opened the scoring on fifteen minutes when he lashed in a shot from the edge of the box after a corner and it stayed one - nil until the start of the second half, then it really kicked off.

Ex Newcastle loanee Howard Gayle brought down Wes Saunders in the box then argued the score about it to such an extent that he was sent off - oh how we chuckled - Beardo duly despatched the kick and we were two - nil up whilst they were down to ten men. Ten minutes later and it happened again, some other makem journeyman (Daniel I think) felling the mighty Kenny Wharton in the area and it was another penalty

So that'd make us three nil up, a Beardsley hatrick and them down to ten men - piece of cake eh? You'd think so wouldn't you, but try to remember we're Newcastle United fans and God likes to take the piss out of us.

Turner saved the penalty, the tackles started flying in and then Colin West (shit player, revered by the inbreds) mis-kicked the ball, making it seem like a delicate chip, and we were suddenly back to two -one. They're pouring forward and we're creaking, Wes Saunders clears one off the line, Jesus what's going on this was meant to be easy? That's why I hate playing these bastards. Luckily, in all of the fighting, blood and snot, everyone had forgotten about our future England star, Sir Peter took a pass off Megson, moved into the area and slotted home three - one, game over.

Well not quite, Gary Bennet, the makem captain, fired into Wes Saunders knee high and rightly got sent off, leaving them with nine men and the Gallowgate End jubilant. A hatrick from Beardsley, two of the makems sent off and three points taken off them plums. As ever the whole ground was magmanimous in victory and we wished our near neighbours all the best for the coming twelve months.

Imagine if you will thirty thousand jubilant Geordie voices chanting as one:-

'HAPPY NEW YEAR'

Fucking magic.

Luton (h) 87-88

This chapter was going to be about a game from the mid to late eighties that featured some horseplay but on reflection I think it was more about one character that day, so you'll have to forgive me if I change the tone slightly and eulogise about one of my first Mag heroes.

As you may have guessed by now, I am not a new breed supporter from the Sky generation. It's fair to say I've served my time on the terraces and have popped up in some far-flung corners of England supporting my team. The likes of Rotherham, Bournemouth, Barnsley and even a little known area called Sunderland were my staple diet of football league grounds 'back in the day' (I wasn't keen on that Sunderland place mind - the locals were a bit thick). So with that in mind you'll have to forgive me if I beat the drum for someone who was never a 'glamour' player, someone who was never likely to beat three men and send a screamer in to the top corner from forty yards and was certainly never going to be famous for his haircut and pop star wife.

No, the bloke in question was what we'd all love to be, a Geordie who got to play for the Toon. Initially starting as a left back he quickly became a cult hero on the Gallowgate end for his fierce tackling, determined attitude and one hundred percent commitment to the Geordie cause. Described in newspaper reports as slightly built, when in reality he was so thin he had to wear weights in his boots when it was windy (his nickname was 'Bones' for fucks sake), his thin frame belied his sheer belief in himself, his team-mates and the Newcastle cause. Step forward...the mighty Kenny Wharton.

He made his debut, aged eighteen, on 24th March 1979 as a sub during a 5-0 defeat away to West Ham and his first team appearances steadily gained in number until he was a mainstay of the promotion team in the 83' season. His career at Newcastle really took off when Jack Charlton arrived at the Toon and started playing him in an advanced midfield role. Big Jack was never a favourite as a manager at Newcastle mainly because of his boring, safety first, style of play (wonder if he was related to Souness?) but the fans were convinced that he'd lost his marbles when he claimed that Kenny 'could play for England'. I was Wharton's biggest fan but even I knew Jack was talking shite.

After Charlton had resigned Kenny stayed in the team under Willie McFaul. He was still booting people up in the air and was a firm terrace favourite but his finest moment was still to come. In the November of this season Newcastle were thrashed four nowt at Kenilworth Road by Luton. I wasn't there but apparently the Hatters took the piss somewhat and were guilty of a bit of 'showboating', something that was duly noted by the Newcastle players. This defeat left us in eighteenth place in Division One (you young lads had better ask your dads to explain the concept of divisions simply numbered one to four). The second of April saw the return match and Newcastle had by now dragged themselves up to mid-table respectability. We'd signed Michael O'Neill from Coleraine in October and he was apparently 'the new George Best' (yup, another one...) but this game was to be the high point of his short career at United.

'Georgie' O' Neill scored a hat-trick and the highly under rated Paul Goddard made it four nowt with a couple of minutes remaining on the clock so some of the United players, recalling what a bunch of posers Luton had been, decided to have some revenge. Darren McDonough (remember him-signed by Keegan and utter shite) clattered young Gazza and from the resulting free kick we strung together four quick passes along the back line with Roeder ending up in possession. We're all cheering (four passes in a row - FOUR, unheard of then) and Glenn does his famous shuffle and then back heels it to Wor Kenny. Bones, realising he has a bit of time and his Geordie heart still bursting with rage at the unnecessary piss taking from the Luton players earlier in the season then sits down on the ball.

Yup, you read that right, in the middle of a first division match Kenny sits on the ball as if totally unconcerned and casually runs his hand through his hair, all he needed was a paper and he could have been sitting on the bog doing his pools coupon.

This only lasts for a couple of seconds, as the Luton players are deeply unhappy. Kenny wasn't daft enough to risk a boot up the arse so he lays it off and then we string together another eight passes all combined with keepy ups and little flicks. This ends when Gazza starts arsing about and Mick Harford attempts to put him in the stand, it's fair to say the Luton players were seriously pissed off and Wor Ken did nowt to dispel this keeping up a steady stream of chat until the end. When the final whistle blows the players all head towards the corner of the Leazes, where the tunnel was at that time, but Steve Foster (big daft, stupid haired, pretend hard man) starts striding towards the grinning Mr. Wharton. Wor Kenny, realising that as he's about five stone lighter than Foster and will probably lose, squares up whilst simultaneously trying to attract the officials and his team mates' attention and the whole thing ended in a melee of players pushing and shoving as they left the field.

That, for me, summed up what Newcastle meant to local boy Kenny Wharton. Luton disrespected the team, his team, and it hurt him so much that five months later it still burned in him and he exacted revenge in the most humiliating way possible for a professional footballer. In August 89', after ten years in the first team and a testimonial attended by over twenty thousand fans, (Rob Lee only got ten thousand) Kenny Wharton was transferred to Carlisle United having played two hundred and sixty eight league games and scoring twenty six league goals for us. He went with mine and the Gallowgate Ends best wishes. He was one of us and always will be...cheers kidda.

Remembering Mad Darren

There are frequent accusations that football these days has sold its soul, that formerly noisy tribal bearpits have become sanitised shadows of their old selves and that baying, committed supporters have become demanding, fickle consumers. I agree with all of that to a certain extent, as I think many supporters, whatever their affiliations, of a certain age would. With this in mind a group of like minded supporters set up the Toon Ultras in a bid to bring back the noise at St. James. It's a worthy aim and I for one hope it succeeds as it seems to me that grounds these days are sterile, Americanised environments, where the main aim is to extract as much cash from the fan/consumer as possible.

But...it wasn't always like that. Back in the eighties St. James Park was a crumbling, old fashioned relic of days gone by. The two main ends were uncovered, seats were a luxury and the toilets were unspeakably bad. The catering would give you botulism, the turnstile operators were bent and todays health and safety police would have a seizure if they witnessed the steps you went up to get to the terraces.

And do you know what...we fucking loved it.

The home end then, if you didn't know, was the Gallowgate and all the boys massed up behind the goal there in one of two sections, The Corner or the Scoreboard. On slow days when the opposition didn't bring many fans we'd amuse ourselves by taunting the residents of whichever section we weren't in and proclaiming our superiority over them. The Scoreboard was so named because of the giant, subbutteo style scoreboard that was erected above the terracing and was visible from all areas of the ground. This used to be climbed by 'over-enthusiastic' and 'tired and emotional' (ie pissed) fans and the letters re-arranged on the rivals teams section to read something abusive.

The amount of times we played 'W A N KE R S', 'T W A T S' and 'G I P P O S' were too numerous to mention but it was very funny, no matter how many times you saw it.

The Corner, so named because it was the corner of the end and led onto the East Stand had a flag planted right at the top of the terracing and just along from it was a little hot dog stand that was robbed left right and centre every other week. It tended to be the preserve of 'blokes', thickly muscled gadgies who had graduated from cutting their teeth in the scoreboard section and held us teenage youngsters in amused disdain, shaking their heads at us... like you do a drunken nephew who's just made a play for the local bike.

To stand on the Gallowgate End on a sunny day, full of beer with thousands of other like minded souls was nearly as good as it got. If the toon were winning or even just playing well then your day was complete.

If it was all going wrong though, if you were on the open terracing in the rain and we were getting a hiding you could always rely on one man.

Mad Darren lived and breathed Newcastle United. You could travel to any toon game, on any day, in any part of the country and he'd be there. He was the type of bloke who planned his life around the fixture list and, once he was at the game, put his heart and soul into it.

I didn't know him to talk to; I didn't even know his real name. I just knew he was Mad Darren and I knew who he was, that was enough. You'd have some beer before the match, get through the turnstile and hurry up the steps; maybe stopping halfway up for a swim in the Gallowgate bogs, then the singing would make you run the last few steps to get in amongst it. You'd hit the scoreboard end and there he'd be, stood on a barrier, swaying drunkenly with the undulations of the crowd around him and you'd join them singing lustily as Darren kept all the terrace favourites rolling off the tongue (that teapot song was a bit weird mind).

To hit a strange town on a dark wintry Saturday or a wet Wednesday night, knowing you'd probably get beat and the locals would be quite keen on re-arranging your face was a daunting task. Sometimes just getting in a bar, having a few pints and then getting to the ground without having to do your Rocky impression was like mission impossible.

But... getting into the match, counting up your fellow travellers in the gloom all the while being taunted by the pig fuckers from whichever crap little shitehole you were in was made worthwhile when a familiar looking figure staggered onto a barrier and proclaimed he was proud to be a Geordie. You knew then it'd be alright and you'd laugh about it later, in fact you might even write about it all one day.

It's fair to say that Mad Darren single handedly kept many of us interested during the shiteness of the late eighties; he was probably also responsible for imbuing in many of us the terrace culture and the love of making a day of it following the mags that exists today.

Sadly, he died in '89 in London following Newcastle at Wimbledon. There was a scuffle with some Wigan Rugby League fans and while the circumstances aren't fully known, the story at the time was that they were mob handed and he was alone. It was a sad end to a young life but, trite as this may sound, he had died as he lived - following his beloved Mags.

No book about Newcastle United would be complete without a tribute To Mad Darren, I was proud to know him, however indirectly, and believe that in a few short years he influenced the lives of more people than many of us will ever meet.

He was the original Toon Ultra.

Everton (a) 88-89

I have a guilty secret, actually it's not mine, in fact, it's not even a secret if you live in the East End of Newcastle. My little brother is a Man Utd fan, has been since he was about six and you can call him all the glory hunting twats you want but you'd be wrong. It all started when they played Arsenal in the seventy nine Cup Final and being competitive brothers we picked a team each. Despite our young age we also had money on the game - serious money...well two pence as I recall (yeah I know what you're thinking but you can fuck off - two pence was loads in the seventies, The Beano was only four pence man!).

For those of you that don't know what happened, Arsenal went two nil up and in the tradition of families all over the world I gave my brother loads of shit. Man Utd did what they normally do and pulled two back near the end and he gave me loads of shit (I was sweating over the money by this time) before Arsenal got the winner with the last kick of the match. A player called Sunderland got the decisive goal ironically enough - there's a good quiz question related to that - but that's about the only good thing related to the word Sunderland...believe me.

So, I've jumped all over him, demanded my loot, spent it on sweets and ate them in front of him - kids eh. To retaliate he, knowing that I'm a fledgling Newcastle supporter, decides he's following Man Utd from now on and, remembering this is way before they were any good mind, proceeds to do so for the rest of his life - awkward little twat.

Just to impress upon me his seriousness in following the Red Devils he took to coming to Newcastle matches with his little pals, standing in the Gallowgate End and actively supporting the other team - whoever that may be. It's fair to say he's taken some stick over the years (and some digs) and rightly so but to his credit - he's always hated Sunderland (not the player - though I did give him good reason) and for that we must give him respect.

Anyway August '88 rolls around; we'd finished in the top ten the previous season and were looking good before the rumours of Gazza wanting to leave started to circulate. He would be the last of the great Geordie players from the eighties to leave the club, Waddle had been the first to jump ship, and soon he was followed by his good mate Peter Beardsley as he looked for a club that had ambition to match his own. Then, in the summer of this year came the hammer blow to every fan and probably was the start of the concerted, and eventually successful, campaign to remove the board of directors at Newcastle.

Paul Gascoigne confirmed the rumours and went to Spurs for just under two million pounds and took with him the hopes of a whole city. The board, perhaps sensing that we weren't best pleased, acted decisively by giving the manager the entire fee to spend and even stuck another million on top for him to play with. Willie McFaul responded by blowing the lot on four players - just four (it wouldn't get you a squad player's big toe these days but back then it was major). It was the biggest splurge in the history of Newcastle United and he hadn't just fired it at anybody, he'd bought real talent and potential. Dave Beasant, the goalkeeper of the moment who had just saved a penalty in the FA Cup final, Andy Thorn, the young brick wall of a centre half who had also won in that final, John Hendrie, highly rated winger coveted by every other club in the land and John Robertson, free scoring Scottish forward that would surely break every goal record going.

As well as that we had youngsters like Ian Bogie, 'the next Gazza', Michael O Neill 'the next George Best' and Darren Jackson 'the next Andy Rivers' (only kidding - obviously he wasn't that good) - this was going to be our year for sure.

Now our first game was away to Everton, who had recently signed Tony Cottee, and I was confident, in fact the whole city was. We were going to have a go at the league title this year without a doubt, three million notes on players, it stood to reason we were going places and the town was buzzing. I even persuaded wor kid to make the journey with me and on the day the atmosphere inside the ground was electric, Everton had a good team then and this would be a good test of our title credentials. As Cottee prepared to kick off someone next to me called him a cockney dwarf and confidently pronounced him as shite and a waste of money - how we all laughed and agreed.

Fifteen seconds later the ball was behind a beaten Dave Beasant and in our net while the shite cockney dwarf wheeled away in celebration of probably the fastest debut goal ever. Ninety minutes later and we were bottom of the league thanks to a hatrick from the aforementioned vertically challenged southern chap. We didn't know it then but we weren't to move from the bottom spot all season and the expensive gamble by the board would ironically be the catalyst for their own removal.

I was narked when we left the ground, particularly with a fifteen year old sibling ripping the piss out of me for daring to think my team might actually win something (it's a pattern that hasn't changed over the years). His enthusiasm for Everton evaporated however, as we came out of the ground to be met by a wall of scousers, no coppers and cries of *'D'yer wanna meet Stanlee...?'*

Luckily for him I'm a forgiving sort and had done this kind of thing before, I grabbed his collar and dragged him at a run through Stanley Park in search of the coaches - I wasn't that worried about the blades or the bin dippers but the thought of what me mam would do to me put an extra spring in my step I can tell you.

*****

Sitting on the coach I took stock of the situation, we'd lost four nowt, we obviously weren't going to win the league and I had a long depressing journey back to Newcastle to look forward to. But, on the plus side my brother and I had finally found something to agree on with regard to football. Getting back into his seat he informed me that he'd changed his mind about cheering for every team that was in opposition to the mags. From that day on there were two permanent inclusions on the combined Rivers hit list, the makems (obviously) and their bitter blue cousins from Merseyside.

Now if I can just get him to wear a Newcastle top when he's pissed...

Liverpool (a) 88-89

Even though it was still early in the season we were looking doomed going into this match. Willie McFaul's master plan was unravelling around us and we were very much in the shite. The season before we'd had Gazza to bail us out, before that Beardsley and prior to him the Waddler, this year we had Mirandinha the first Brazilian to play in the football league.

We all loved Mira and to be fair he loved us, but the plain fact is he wasn't good enough and didn't really like the cold which, let's face it, is something we have lots of in Newcastle. In an effort to encourage him though we'd given him his own song:-

We've got Mirandinha
He's not from Argentina
He's from Brazil
He's fucking brill

Repeat and jump around ...

George Michael must have been shitting himself.

Gazza's departure to Spurs had left a gaping hole in our team that we'd struggled to fill. Local boy Ian Bogie had given it a go but come up short despite the constant talking him up in the local press as being better than Gascoigne it was obvious he wasn't up to it and this was illustrated by his career being spent mostly in the lower leagues.

So McFaul's bold gamble on selling Gazza and keeping the cash out of the pockets of the board was looking a bit silly now. Our record transfer prior to this was a quarter of a million pounds on John Trewick (yeh I know - but fuck off he was alright man) but, despite smashing it with our four new signings, we were bang in trouble.

I've highlighted already that it wasn't working and that we were going down, in the main this was really down to McFaul. He'd been with the club for over twenty years and was a likeable bloke. Also in his favour was that he was our goalkeeper when we'd last won something (The Fairs cup in 1969, the year before I was born - not that I'm the jinx you understand) in fact he was very much an adopted Geordie. None of this however made him a good manager and his fatal mistake was to try something new buoyed by our good showing the year before. He introduced the three - five - two formation to Newcastle and got it wrong...badly wrong.

Opposing teams would just play everything down the wings wait for one of our lumbering centre halves to sell himself short and they were in. The mistake was eventually corrected and we went back to a more regular formation but by then the damage was done. Morale was shattered, the players stopped believing in the manager, the cockney press gleefully labelled us a 'crisis' club (nowt changes eh) and we were set for a long slow death.

The irony of it all really was that this season saw the introduction of the 'supporters for change' group which ultimately led to The Hall family getting into the seat of power at St. James and also introduced the first strains of the, now nationally popular, 'sack the board' chant. The ironic thing is that basically the board had done what the fans had wanted and given McFaul loads of cash to spend and he'd blown it. If they'd reverted to type and given him twenty five pence and a pickled egg then he wouldn't have tried the continental fancy dan stuff and we'd have had a boring, mid-table season. This would have resulted in John Hall and his ilk not getting in and none of the magnificent Keegan years, so really we've got a lot to thank Gordon McKeag for.

Anyway the match, we were lambs to the slaughter. The pundits had us down as cannon fodder, it was a game for the mighty Liverpool to increase their goal difference and we were simply bit part players in the main act. Unfortunately for the 'experts' we're Newcastle United and we don't do what is expected of us - ever.

We went one-nil up, John Hendrie cutting in from the angle and squeezing in a shot at the far post. Not to worry, the mighty reds would soon put the upstarts in their place - yep here we go one all. Now you'll see some goals, well no actually, the lads dug in, David McCreery hit everything that moved and we ground out what was looking increasingly like a draw as the minutes ticked down until...we got a penalty...at the Kop End...

No-one ever got a penalty at Liverpool in those days, after the match the referee was probably blacklisted and sent to work in the Conference league for that faux pas, and we were all unsure as to who was even going to take it.Then one man stepped forward. A man who's every touch, pass and shot since his history making move to English football had been monitored and criticised.

A man who apparently had a 'fragile temperament' and a 'questionable attitude'.

A man with a point to prove.

Our Brazilian magician stood over the ball as the entire cast of Bread and the Liver Birds tried to put him off, they screamed abuse, they made threatening gestures and they waved their massive taches' at him, surely the fragile psyche of our diminutive import would crack? Not a chance - he calmly slotted it home and then, in a gesture for which he is remembered and loved by Geordies of a certain age even today, he ran towards the Kop kissing his Newcastle badge and laughing at them. What a bloke.

As you know we went down that year and we were shit but mighty Liverpool, the darlings of the media, couldn't beat us home or away. For a lad who lived on a shitty council estate and had prospects more meagre than those of a mackem at a top models convention then that would have to do.

Arsenal (h) 88-89

Ever heard of David Robinson? No? Well let me illustrate the difference between how good professional footballers actually are and, despite what we all claim in the pub after another nil - nil draw, why we could never be one. In the early eighties I'd gone to Benfield Comprehensive school, it had a good reputation then, I don't know about now but it was well thought of back in the days of only three television channels. The school has spawned a couple of pro footballers in its time, the likes of Steve Bruce (Man Utd through and through no matter what he claims), Lee Clark, Dave Roach and David Robinson to name a few from the top of my head. You'll have heard of Bruce and Clark, Roachy played quite a few times in the first team under Ossie Ardiles before Keegan moved him on and Robinson, recognise that name?

Well he made his first team debut in this game after coming up through the ranks and made a number of substitute appearances, scoring one goal, before dropping down the divisions. The general consensus on the Gallowgate End (and bear in mind we were shite then) was that he just wasn't good enough for us at a time when we were a second division team.

This match did little to change anyone's opinion of him, basically it, and he, was shite. We lost by one goal to nil (the original Alan Smith if my memory serves me right) and the Arsenal fans got to sing their famous chant. Anyone who wasn't around then and has only seen the modern day Gooners ply their premiership trade would not believe it was the same club. They revelled in playing defensive football and practiced their offside trap like Robbie Savage practices being annoying. In short, their whole attitude, style of play and purpose for existing as a football club has changed as radically in the last twenty years as the whole concept of taking the telephone from the shelf in the house and carrying it around in your pocket.

Anyway, we got beat, it was boring and Robinson was judged as no good on his very first appearance. I agreed loudly and vociferously with all the blokes around me at the time, well you do when you're seventeen and full of beer don't you, but all the while I was harbouring a guilty secret and a private animosity towards 'Robbo'.

I'd played in direct opposition to him in a school match only a couple of years previously. He was the star striker in our year's 'A' team while I was one of two plodding centre halves in the 'B' team. Incidentally I think our manager just picked us both together for a laugh, my defensive sidekicks' name was Fish (alright Mickey, hope you're well) and my mine is obviously Riv.. well you get the picture. Actually there was a bloke in the squad called Waters as well, I kid you not.

Anyway, every season there was a 'friendly' match between the then first and second teams on a Friday afternoon before the big kick off, this was always well attended as it got you out of lessons for the rest of the day and if you were crafty you could sneak off early to start your weekend. So, young Dave had recently cracked getting into the Newcastle United youth team and I'd be marking him, this was it, this was the year I'd be making my claim to an 'A' team spot and recognition from the scouts that always came to Benfield. My rightful place in the football league was assured after I sorted this big headed twat out, I couldn't wait for the kick off. As the sun shone down brightly on the whole school and a gentle breeze casually touched the tops of the blades of brilliant green grass I went over my strategy. Hit him hard early on, beat him to the first ball every time, make him look a twat, get promoted to the 'A' team, get scouted, use my muscular frame to win a contract at the toon as a top centre half, live on easy street. Piece of piss.

The ref, resplendent in his all black football league gear (he was a genuine league referee) raised his whistle to his lips and looked at both goalkeepers. The whistle went and I strode into battle...ten minutes later and we were three nil down, Robbo had a hatrick and he'd been told to ease off by the PE teacher. At the end they won something like eight-nil, he'd got five and never really broken sweat, I couldn't get near him, I tried to kick him, nut him, punch him, everything but was made to look a mug every time, maybe I should have tried kicking the ball.

Anyway, next time you're in the boozer moaning about how Lampard's not good enough for England and Neville's a load of shite, just remember, they're much, much better than Dave Robinson, he was much, much better than me...and well...I'm probably much, much better than you, so think on.

Last I heard he was working as a copper somewhere - hope he doesn't read this.

Man Utd (a) 88-89

We were down well before this match was even on the horizon. If the truth be known we were relegated pretty much from the first kick of the season when Cottee ('over-rated cockney dwarf' - knowledgeable fans eh?) scored after fifteen seconds at Everton. Apart from a few glorious backs to the wall, dig in and kick everything that moves type efforts we'd been dire for nine months and we knew it. The thing was though, the thing no-one in this new Sky era would understand, is that even though we knew early on that we were finished we never gave up. The fans turned up singing every week and did their best to lift the team and occasionally, just every now and then, it worked.

This wasn't one of those games though, Willie McFaul had been dispensed with halfway through the season and replaced by 'wily old veteran' Jim Smith. His main tactic to save us was to put ten men behind the ball and hope for the best, oh that and alienating all of our best young players. The likes of Darren Jackson and Michael O Neill who had been immense in the previous season were cast aside by the bald eagle and replaced by older journeymen and guess what? It didn't work.

For this match we were actually mathematically down, the worst team in the division with thirty one points (still nowhere near as bad as the makems though in both of their record breaking seasons - lest we forget) and popular opinion had it that we would be having a go at the mighty reds in this game. Actually, I say the mighty reds but, and for those of you who hadn't heard of football before the aforementioned Sky television told you what to think and do, this might come as a bit of a shock, they weren't that good then.

Honestly, Man Utd in the late eighties under the early stewardship of Sir Alex Ferguson were nothing more than a midtable team - they finished this particular campaign in eleventh with fifty one points, indeed a lot of the stalwart red army wanted Ferguson out at that time. Oh and the next time they start giving it that where were you when you were shit nonsense you could point out to them that this game had an attendance of thirty seven thousand with conservative estimates of the Newcastle following being between ten and fifteen thousand - maybe the prawn sandwiches weren't as good then eh?

Anyway, the game itself. We were surely going to go for the jugular in what looked like being our last game in the top division for quite some time weren't we? Nope, one man up front, the other ten behind the ball and let's try to keep the score down lads. Fuck the big mob of Geordies that have spent half a week's wages on trains and beer, we'll just hope for the best eh.

I would have been furious but for one thing, I wasn't there.

Unfortunately for me, the night before I'd had a few pints too many and had an altercation with a bus stop window. Well, it wasn't actually me that had the argument with it but one of my mates, we all ended up in Clifford Street nick though. By the time I got home and sorted myself out I'd well and truly missed my bus - on reflection though sometimes you have to be thankful for small mercies.

My mate eventually got a thirty quid fine and was asked how he intended to pay, he was renowned as a tight fucker and asked if he could pay a pound a week. The judge pondered on this and came back with the immortal line 'This isn't a catalogue bill young man.'

Quality stuff from the judge but not so from the team or the manager. We ended the game two- nil down without a recognised striker actually playing, poor reward for the travelling fans that'd paid a lot of money to follow a shit team all season and do you know what? They still applauded the fuckers off, sang the managers name and told the Man United fans 'We'll meet again' at the end - even now it brings a tear to the eye.

Leeds (h) 89-90

One of the most famous debuts in the magnificent and chequered history of Newcastle United was that of Mickey Quinn. As you all know (or you bloody should) he blasted four past the might of big spending Leeds United, that season's favourites to win the Second division, and in the process undermined a whole stay away campaign aimed at ousting the then board of directors. That night the entire city had the same song booming out from every pub.

'Come on without, come on within...You'll not see nothing like the Mighty Quinn.'

You know the song, you remember the game and you definitely remember the goals. So do I right? Wrong. I wasn't there and it wasn't because of any campaign either.

The week before the season began I'd decided to take a break from my labouring job in a steel factory. My cousin Paul, my mate Spadge and me had decided to get away from it all in Blackpool. There's not a lot to report on the actual holiday, well, if you discount getting thrown our of our digs, having to tout our tickets for Chubby Brown on the seafront to pay for another Bed and Breakfast and Spadge getting blown out by every lass within a twenty mile radius. Aye, apart from that it was quite uneventful but the journey back...well that was a different story.

Picture the scene, three lads wearing stupid 'kiss me quick' hats and carrying blue golf umbrellas (always get an umbrella in Blackpool - it's never sunny) talking excitedly about the match as their train back to Geordieland pulls into York station. Comments like 'not long noo' and 'I cannit wait for a decent pint me instead of this southern shite' booming from their young mouths. Then picture them going silent as the platform hoves into view. Hundreds upon hundreds of massive, thickly muscled (or fat - think Chris Moyles), Leeds fans are bouncing, chanting and jigging about on the platform.

No more jokes about 'Yorkshire puddings', no more digs at 'soft southern bastards' just a grim faced, silent battle of nerves. Spadge goes missing - he's older than us and looks like a student anyway. Me and Paul stand out, too stupid to take off the hats and melt into the background. You've heard of being 'the grey man' it's what spooks and special forces types do, you never notice them. Well me and Paul weren't so much the grey men as the 'luminous pink with blue spots men' and yet, somehow, we were getting away with it. We stood by the door, backs against it and cases behind our legs so the main body of Leeds couldn't see us, we grunted at the odd straggler who came by for a piss or a British Rail sandwich and we were really and truly getting away with it. Our tactics were sorted for when we pulled into Central Station, cases under our arms and head for the taxi bays sharpish. We got closer, got past Durham. Not long now. Piece of piss. Leeds? Fuck all mate.

Then a copper, one of two on the whole train, came by.

'You won't get into the match with those brollies lads' he opined.

Time stood still as the odd couple of Leeds lads looked over sympathetically at two of 'their own' being harassed by plod, the sympathy didn't last long like, thanks to numbnuts next to me.

'Wa not gannin to the match yet - wa gannin yem first man - we've been on holider to Blackpool.'

His voice tailed off as he reached the end of his sentence and he realised what he'd just done, I cringed inwardly and the copper just looked dumbstruck at having to now earn his overtime. The Leeds contingent around us fought each other to get down the carriage to tell their mates that there was a bit of target practice just waiting to be hit in the corridor. By the time a little crew of them had surrounded us we had the other copper in attendance and were fending them off with the umbrellas.

We took a few digs, lots of spit and many more insults. As the train pulled into the Station we were off like rabbits round Brough Park, case under one arm, poking the brollies behind us with the other. It was like a carry on film but the only tits on show were wearing fucking 'Kiss me quick' hats. As we approached the taxi rank, there was only one car and some selfish twat was already in it.

'Taaxxxiii'

'Shite we're in bother noo'

I could smell the sweaty, fat, Tetleys drinkers behind me and hear the 'Leeds, Leeds, Leeds' chants reverberating off the walls of one of Englands finest railways stations. As I ran for my life I considered that at least there was plenty of coppers about as well as medical staff to tend to me following my imminent kicking. Then big gob next to me broke into my thoughts with...'No we're not - it's Spadge in the taxi'

We dived in, simultaneously calling him a bottling twat and telling the driver to get his foot down. As we pulled away though Spadge redeemed himself by bravely giving them the V's - what a hero. Anyway, as a result we missed the match, borrowed some cash and went on the drink in the safety zone of Byker, we listened to the match on the radio in the boozer and cheered every time Quinny poked another one past them.

Altogether now...Come on without...

Leicester (h) 89-90

We had some mental games against Leicester in the early nineties, there's obviously both the famous seven-one and the relegation threatened two-two draw under Keegan but this was the first of the amazing sequence of games that took you on a ninety minute roller coaster ride. This is probably made all the more remarkable by the fact that Leicester just aren't the first team you think of these days when you hear the words Newcastle, goals and excitement. But believe me, this game would easily live up to, and even surpass, any other in that respect.

It all started innocuously enough. A mid season clash between two poor second division teams doesn't exactly get the blood racing, but we needed the points to stay in touch with the promotion pack and Jim Smith had probably played his last card with the purchase of Scotland captain Roy 'The Bear' Aitken, another veteran player to join his ageing team.

Aitken's arrival promised at least a little stability at the back of the team and we looked forward to letting in less goals if nothing else but his first contribution was actually a positive one. He surged forward from the back to feed Fereday (God I still have nightmares about him) who, for once, crossed the ball and Mark McGhee put us one up. The Corner went mad, particularly me, Col and our Paul. Him and me were off to work at Butlins in Ayr for six months not long after this so it was a bit of an all day piss up for us and we decided that the lads obviously knew this and wanted to send us off in style.

That thought didn't last long; Leicester equalised soon after and took control, our old failings beginning to surface as we struggled to keep up with them. I was still grafting in the steel factory at this point and making good money so confidently predicted a draw and said we should get off at half time and get on the lash. Then we got a penalty and I changed my mind...Kevin Dillon got into the City box and instead of just blazing it into the Leazes End as he normally would, he somehow managed to fall over Hodge in the Leicester goal and fluke a penalty.

'Get in Kev - I never called you a crap mackem...nah man not me...ever'...as you can see dear reader nowt changes, the banter was as hilarious then as it is now.

Super Johnny Anderson who could hit the ball harder than George Best could hit the drink stepped up to take it and we knew it would be two one...well until the keeper saved it anyway. Then they went up the field and scored before we managed to level right on half time. The much maligned (by me anyway) Mark Stimson crossing for the Mighty Quinn to belt one home. We were going nowhere now and, deciding that we could hoy them down our necks two at a time later on to get us to the level of drunkenness needed to approach the lasses we normally attracted, we vowed to stay until the death.

The second half kicked off and Gary McAllister (remember him) took control, scoring one then setting up another to put us four two down and making our decision look a little bit daft as the skies darkened. Aitken looked pissed off as he realised what he'd just joined and the crowd mentally wrote off yet another expensive defensive acquisition (and it wouldn't be the last time we'd do that would it?)

John Gallacher entered the fray, Hughie's grandson, as he was known on the terraces, was a crafty winger in the old 'Jinky' Scottish style and he soon changed the game. He got hold of a McGhee flick and made it four three with ten minutes left. We were screaming 'attack, attack' and Aitken got his head up again and started pumping his fists at his new teammates. Brock floated in a corner, Liam O Brien nodded on and the Mighty Quinn poked home his second of the match before running to the Corner in celebration. We, obviously, went mental and shouted for the ref to 'blow your fucking whistle man' before they could go and score again when the unthinkable happened...we only got the winner.

McGhee got the ball on the edge of their box and stupidly ignoring my clever tactical advice to 'take it to the corner' he unprofessionally rounded two defenders and buried it in the net. I forgave him this amateur approach as I bounced up and down the terracing with thousands of other people I didn't know but made a mental note to write to the club and ask them to have a word with him.

Amazingly enough, when we played at Leicester in the very next season it finished five four down there but to them this time, a certain Mr. David Kelly getting a hatrick for them and a young Mr. Quinn getting one for us.

So next time we have to play them and it's raining and you can't be bothered and you're thinking of maybe staying in the boozer or slipping off early to start your night out - don't. You might think that Leicester just means Gary Linekers ears and crisps but it doesn't.

Leicester equals goals - loads of them.

YOU'RE TWISTING ME MELON MAN

The Nineties

Peterborough (a) 92-93

You know how it is when your team has just survived relegation and probable bankruptcy by the skin of their teeth and then spent a few quid in the summer on class players that you never thought in a million years would sign for them?

Yeah? You know that feeling?

Well after that do you know the feeling of winning your first seven games in a row, particularly against opposition that's expected to top your league - the likes of West Ham and big spending Derby County spring to mind - you know that feeling as well aye? Well if you do then you'll understand how I came to be in a transit van heading for a town I'd barely heard of, and certainly didn't know where it was, on a very sunny Saturday morning with a hangover that screamed 'kill me now and make it stop.'

Our season had kicked off so well and had gone so smoothly that as Newcastle fans we knew, we just knew, the wheels would come off at some point and so we had to celebrate every weekend as if we'd just won the league before it all went to rat shit. Hence my hangover and my drunken insistence the night before that we go to Peterborough and support the lads - this wasn't an all ticket match as the authorities hadn't caught on yet and so you could still make these decisions when you were drunk on a Friday after you'd been paid. Col, as sympathetic as ever, obviously noticed my painfully contorted facial expression as the sun beamed in through the van windscreen and lasered holes into my already aching skull and stated the obvious.

'Telt you not to drink the drambuie didn't I?'

'Aye'

'Said you were making a knob of yourself didn't I?

59

'Aye'

'Do you want a can?'

'Aye'

I fucking love away games me.

When we got there I discovered that Peterborough is a nice place with a pleasant town centre and a ground by the river. I also discovered that half of Newcastle had obviously had the same idea as me the night before and had mobbed the place.

We couldn't get into a boozer and get served to save our lives, you couldn't even get in the doors of most of them but that was mainly because the tab machines and bandits were coming out. A lot of publicans made a lot of money that day but I'm fairly sure a lot insurance companies made some big vending and gambling machine related payouts the following week. We cut our losses, headed to a supermarket we'd noticed and bought some cans then laid down by the river and bathed in the sunshine whilst necking them. The locals seemed entranced by our presence, it was almost as if they had woken up that day and realised all the animals at the local safari park had got loose and were on the streets where they lived.

Reports differed on how many Geordies were in town but you can take my word as gospel on this one - basically it was all of us, there was no-one left in the toon at all. At about two o clock, Mickey, our more experienced travelling companion and designated driver, decreed that we should head to the ground or we wouldn't get in. We obviously deferred to the wisdom of the older man by moaning that he was being boring cos he couldn't have a drink but followed him anyway...I was glad we did. The ground was chocker, massive queues snaked back for what seemed like miles and they were all Geordies, going in all ends. We jumped in the van, drove to Aberdeen, joined what looked like the shortest line and started praying, luckily we had a couple of cans left to offset the fear of not getting in and even more luckily, we made it ...just.

The turnstiles stopped behind us after about five more lads had come in and we took that as an omen and headed up the stairs - it was bedlam. Our end was covered, a cow shed affair if you like and it was rammed, you couldn't move. The noise was incredible and, I kid you not, the condensation due to our body heat was dripping back on us from the roof beams overhead. It was like being in a rave and it was fucking brilliant.

The teams came out together, we were led by Barry Venison and he came out with his fists in the air, his arms pumping and a look in his eye that said 'have you seen all them in that stand - we're fucking having this today'. Obviously I'm paraphrasing, he might just have had a bit of grit in there or something but you get the picture.The game itself wasn't brilliant, it didn't need to be. We won through a Sheedy goal from an inch perfect pass by a recently acquired Robert Lee and that was enough. The team, the fans and, indeed our whole city, was once again fighting for each other and it had been demonstrated to the entire football world that day in a little Southern town in the back of beyond - and we were there, revelling in it.

Mind you me head was still knacking when we got back in the van like.

Barnsley (h) 92-93

I thought, at the time, that this was the best game I would ever see involving Newcastle United. I was wrong, as you'll see later on, but that shouldn't denigrate from the way we tore Barnsley apart.

The day had started well for me anyway, my mate Rob had spent the season working for the firm who had taken over the catering at St. James a while back. As he was well in with the boss he used to get access to those luminous sticker things that got you in as a pie seller and, in Byker, he was a very popular man to say the least. He'd rung me earlier in the day to let me know I'd be getting in gratis so I quickly offloaded the season ticket (face value - proper old school me) and nipped over to my local, the Stag's Head in Byker, to prepare.

*****

I met him by the main doors of the ground and he ushered me in. All the way up the steps I expected a hand on my shoulder and a boot up my arse but, amazingly, the door was held open for me, Rob slapped the sticker onto my chest and then uttered the immortal words 'got a bit of a surprise for you son.' I blindly followed him through a couple of doors and then into a dark corridor, it was almost tunnel like...hold on that's the 'Howay the Lads' sign...fuck me, I'm in the tunnel.

I'M IN THE TUNNEL!

By the time I'd taken this in we were coming out of the other end and thousands of early birds craned their necks to see who this new arrival was.

'He looks like Mickey Quinn'

'Nah Quinny's not that fat.'

Cheeky fuckers.

I gave a little wave just to prolong the schoolboy fantasy and then it was over. I jumped into the middle paddock to the left of the tunnel, ripped my sticker off and blended in - nearly match time.

And what a match it was.

We battered them, properly and without mercy. Everytime we got the ball their defenders shook like shitting dogs. Lee Clark, Rob Lee and Scott Sellars buzzed about everywhere, picking up the ball, running with it and attacking incessantly. They were mirror images of their manager in his playing days and we lapped it up. Their industry and scheming, combined with the predatory finishing skills of our hot new striker, Andy Cole, led to us giving Barnsley a proper hiding. We did them six nil on a night when Cole got a hatrick, Sellars opened his account (he would soon get another, much more important goal against a certain team from down the road) and John Beresford, already a crowd hero got his only goal for the toon and celebrated like he'd just won the pools.

At the end the scoreboard simply read 'Pure Geordie Magic' and they were spot on.

Rotherham (a) 92-93

It started on the Friday night before the match. We'd got Rotherham in the FA Cup and were absolutely pissing the first division. We were certs to go up to the new Premiership. Incidentally here's a question for you, on the first day of the brand new all singing all dancing Premier Division which ground had the highest attendance of the day in England?

Was it Man U? Liverpool? Chelsea? Everton or Spurs? Was it fuck. It was the team that finished fifth bottom of the old second division just eight weeks before - Newcastle United.

And who were we playing that day? Some crack continental outfit or travelling South American team? No it was fucking Southend. So next time you're at St. James and the usual suspects are singing 'where were you when you were shit' just laugh at them, cos we were where we always were, in the Gallowgate End in the rain, while they were at home watching Sky.

Anyway, as I say, the Keegan revolution was in full swing and we were doing well. Rotherham away should present us with no problem on our road to glory and tickets were hard to come by. We'd been unable to get them and had resigned ourselves to not going when, in the Stag's the night before the match, we'd managed to get ourselves two tickets for a fiver each. The only problem being that they were forgeries and the police knew that they were changing hands.

'Fuck it, who dares wins' we'd said, pissed up, and bought them, handing over another fiver each for the privilege of travelling in someone's transit van. The last thing I remember about that night was Smudger's closing words to us as Col and me danced round the juke box at midnight 'Be here at eight, if you're late you don't go. No refunds lads.'

'Aye Smudge, nee bother,' we shouted back mortal drunk and continued knocking back the shorts.

At ten to eight me mam must have let Col in as at nine and a half minutes to eight he was swilling my head under the sink in the bathroom and shouting at me to get dressed. At thirty seconds to eight we were outside the pub and the van was nowhere to be seen.

At ten past eight, having gone to the shop at the bottom of the road for a can of coke and a paper we noticed a white transit heading down the street towards us. It pulled up next to the pub and Smudge sauntered out saying 'You're early lads, we're not meeting till half eight. You a bit keen to get on the drink then?' I nearly cried. Firstly at the thought I could have had another half hour in bed and secondly at the mention of the word 'drink'. It was all I could do to keep my coke down when Col mentioned going back to me mam's for a bacon sandwich.

When we finally got in the van I was relieved to see that there were some rudimentary seats in the back made out of packing cases and I settled down for a kip, that lasted until we picked up the other ten lads and got packed into what was fast becoming an airless, humid hell on earth. We hit Yorkshire just as my hangover really took hold and I was forced to start drinking to numb the pain, buying a fourpack off one of the lads who'd overstocked.

By the time we got to Rotherham I was well up for it again, the four cans of lager topping up my Cointreau and Vodka concoction from the night before. Of the thirteen of us in the van we all had forged tickets but I was confident we'd get in no bother.

After a few, incident free pints round town we headed for the match and this was where it started to unravel. The rumour of forged tickets was common knowledge in Newcastle so it stands to reason that the South Yorkshire bizzies would be aware of it and they'd basically erected a mounted barrier of coppers before the Newcastle turnstiles and were checking as many tickets as possible as you walked past them.

The consensus was to quickly split up and crumple and dirty our tickets up so they looked half reasonable, good thinking, we all got past the mounted bizzies. Laughing to myself I approached the turnstile and handing my ticket over I pushed against it. It didn't move so I pushed again, still nowt and then I was aware of the turnstile operator saying 'No way pal, that's a forgery.' I snatched it back and tried the next one along and then the next one and then the next one...bollocks.

Looking along the street outside the away end it seemed that I was the only one of us who'd been caught, everyone else was in and I was in Rotherham on my own on match day. Fucking marvellous. I was just trying to remember where the nearest pub was in relation to the van when a hand came out of nowhere and grabbed my shoulder 'Got a forged ticket have you son?' Brilliant, not only missing the match but nicked as well, cursing myself for not just throwing it away when I was knocked back at the turnstiles I turned round saying 'No officer I appear to have lost it and..'

Looking back at me with a big grin on his face was one of the lads from the van, a regular from Jacksons on Shields Road.

'Howay, Andy isn't it? Follow me son, I've got a plan.'

So, being young and naive I followed him...all the way round to the home end.

The queues weren't that big in their end, mainly because it was all ticket so people thought they could take their time in the pub. We just joined the smallest queue and kept quiet while all around us South Yorkshires finest slagged off Geordies. I let my newest mate go first when we got to the front and watched amazed as he slapped a fiver down on the counter, mouthed something at the bloke, motioned back to me and then jumped the turnstile. I just followed him as quick as possible, hoyed a fiver at the turnstile bloke and we were in.

'This is the plan,' he said, 'we'll give it half an hour and then tell a copper we're Geordies in the wrong end, they'll take us up to the Newcastle section and we're laughing.'

It sounded okay to me, I wasn't too keen on watching the match surrounded by these bastards. When you think of them in a football sense you think of 'little Rotherham perennial football league strugglers' and 'playing Newcastle? Oh the romance of the cup'. Well all I could see was big, fifteen stone, pie eating nutters covered in tattoos and no matter how much aftershave they'd slapped on there'd be no fucking romance going on there I can tell you.

Anyway, come twenty to three we've had enough of being quiet and as we edge to the front we tell a copper who we are, he just points us to a corner of the stand we're in and tells us to go in there. Now, basically it's a taped off area at one side of the old cow shed that doubles as the home end and there's about fifteen Geordies in there and two coppers looking after us. The home fans were none too pleased at this point as they were getting crushed to fuck while we stretched out looking longingly at the massed ranks of Geordies at the other end. The way the black and white tops swayed drunkenly in the sun singing lustily and chanting abuse was just wonderful, if only we could be in there.

Instead we were in the home end and things were getting nasty, the yorkies were wanting their space back and telling the coppers so, they were also aiming punches and spit over the tape while plod turned a blind eye. The usual throat slitting gestures were being aimed at us and, as me and my new mate (who I'd just worked out was a heed the ball) looked like the most likely lads, we seemed to be on the receiving end of most of them. I was shitting myself. My new pal though? He laughed at them and said things like 'when you're ready lads' and blew them kisses.

Something had to give and at five to three it did. The already packed in Yorkshire crowd was added to by a sudden surge of drunken latecomers and our police line was breached.

This gave the agitators the excuse they needed and they poured across the terracing into us. I had swung a punch, been hit and was already over the barrier and onto the pitch when I looked back and saw my newest compadre fighting with two of them. My natural cowardice battled with my conscience as I weighed up the pro's and cons of helping him.

Sighing to myself I jumped back into the stand ready to be knocked out when luckily a copper grabbed me and threw me out onto the pitch closely followed by my laughing nutter mate all swollen knuckles and cut face. Result, I thought as the relief flooded my body; in the match, didn't get a hiding and now we get to go in the right end.

As we were escorted around the side of the pitch to the Newcastle end the players were already out and I swear 'Killer' Kilcline gave me the thumbs up. Then, when we approached the Newcastle end they rose as one and acclaimed us while we waved at them. Bear in mind that all they'd saw was fifteen of us fighting off thousands of them (or swinging wildly whilst screaming 'not the face, not the face' in my case). In the old seventies tradition we'd nearly 'taken their end' and that deserved praise.

As we entered our end to chants of 'hero, hero' I looked up at the swaying, mass of my extended family. I was part of this, I belonged, and in (nearly) the words of one of our finest managers I loved it...I really fucking loved it.

The match? Oh we drew 1-1, beat them in the replay and went out in the next round.

<u>Leicester (h) 92-93</u>

This whole season had been amazing, I'd seen nothing like it in my life. I pretty much knew we were going up as early as the third game of the campaign, obviously being Newcastle we could still have managed to snatch defeat from the jaws of victory, but I'd simply ignored that possibility and had spent the whole season grinning like Victoria Beckham every time Dave's wage slip came through the post. Even the season we'd been promoted with Keegan the player hadn't compared to this, then it had been a roller coaster ride where we'd sneaked into third place purely by scoring loads of goals but this time...I'd even been sure of us finishing as champions by about Christmas. This was the final match, at home to Leicester, we had been confirmed as champs the week before courtesy of beating Grimsby two - nil at their own ground; a match that had seen more Newcastle fans in the ground (and on the pitch) than the locals and now it was party time.

Keegan had filled the whole city with belief and confidence, the place was on a high and everywhere you looked there was a black and white shirt. This attitude was magnified on match days when the team played some magnificent football with a swagger and panache and this final match of the season was to be no exception. I took my place on the Gallowgate Terraces for the last time, I had a season ticket for the new Leazes End stand for next season and my concrete stepped home of the last ten years would be replaced before I had another chance to say goodbye. The atmosphere was fantastic, the whole ground, in fact as I mentioned before, the whole city, was rocking. You could smell the beer, hear the laughter and just feel the good vibe around the whole place as we prepared to take on a team that had nearly sent us into Division Three just twelve months earlier. As the teams ran out to a mighty roar my match day companions turned up. They looked fantastic in their Oxfam suits, painted with Black and White stripes and they were greeted with much applause by the rest of the Scoreboard, unfortunately, as they'd been up most of the night applying the stripes, the paint hadn't had time to dry so the cheers soon turned to good natured abuse.

Me? I kept at least two feet away, when you're going straight out from the match (as about ninety nine percent of the crowd were) then you don't want paint on your pulling gear.

Leicester City weren't a bad team; they were in the play offs and had a chance of making the Premier League. They were a solid outfit managed by a good, professional, tactician and had come prepared for a hard game.

We fucking destroyed them in forty five minutes.

At half time it was six - nil to Newcastle and could have been more. We'd seen a David Kelly hat-trick, two from Andy Cole (when he gets the ball he scores a goal) and a corker from Rob Lee (scores a goal on the ITV). Leicester were shell-shocked, the telly companies were orgasmic at the show we were putting on and the fans? Well man, we were used to it.

Nah, only kidding, we were going mental every time any-one scored, pitch invasions, new songs, victory dances, it was class and I never wanted it to end. The second half saw Andy Cole complete his hat-trick and a Leicester consolation got the biggest cheer of the day.

Before that though, two things happened at half time that stick in my mind, one changed my life and the other, well, that just filled my belly which, at the end of the day is just as impor-tant to a fifteen stone chancer from Byker.

We were discussing the previous half excitedly and I was trying to get black and white paint off my strides when I heard someone shout my name. I looked up and my mate Rob was coming off the touchline and into the scoreboard towards me. The whole crowd was watching as he handed me a hot dog wrapped in foil with the words 'you'll need this if you're stopping oot son - see you later on.' And then he was off. My neighbours looked on in amazement as I shouted after him 'Tell John Hall this new delivery service will never work mind - me hotdog's cold.'

The second thing happened soon after when Chris, the eldest brother of my two pals, casually asked me if I'd ever worked away before?

'Oh aye, I did six months at a Butlins camp in Scotland'

'Can you use a tape measure?'

'Aye' (well I'd never really had any cause to use one before but how hard could it be?)

'I'm taking some lads to Barcelona to work as chippies - do you fancy coming along as a labourer? I'll give you two hundred quid a week in your hand and you'll get your flights and digs for nowt - what do you reckon - do you fancy it?'

Now obviously this had to be carefully considered, I mean, I was pissed, high on the match and generally in a good mood so it would be easy to just get caught up in it and say yes without thinking it through.

'Fucking right I fancy it.'

'One other thing, you'll have to pretend to be a joiner if anyone asks, just cut something every time a gaffer walks past. Think you can manage it?'

'Piece of piss.'

So my parameters changed and my horizons widened as about four weeks later I hit Spain and realised quickly that not everyone in the world spoke English. From there it was a series of small discoveries about myself culminating in the realisation that I had learnt Spanish quickly and without a problem. Then, whilst bemoaning the crap novels I was reading on the beach during my dinner breaks (better than sitting in the works canteen eh?) I caught onto the fact that maybe, just maybe, a scrote from a council estate could start thinking about things like writing books himself.

Spurs & Sheff Wed (h) 93-94

I'd been in Spain for a couple of months when the first game of our debut premier league season rolled around and with true football mysticism and coincidence it threw up an intriguing prospect.

As well as the fear that maybe we'd struggle in the big boys league and the possibility we'd all got a bit carried away with ourselves and our 'look out Man Utd cos we're coming through' predictions we had another reason to be a bit reticent. Ossie Ardiles, Keegans predecessor, was coming back and he was bringing a highly rated Tottenham team with him. It would be a stern test of our Premiership credentials. Luckily I wouldn't have to bite my nails as someone else would be using my shiny new season ticket while I was still in Barcelona.

I don't know if you've ever been there but it's a top city and as it was my first time abroad ever (hey, I had a deprived childhood alright) it did, and still does, fascinate me.

I was used to being out on the drink at six on a weekend (well if it wasn't an all dayer) and in a club by eleven but here they didn't go out until then. As you can imagine it took me a while to get over this culture shock and many's the Saturday night I was mortal by midnight with another six hours of drinking to go and the sound of 'crazy eenglish' ringing in my ears. Mind you I much preferred the tapas idea rather than necking kebabs at two in the morning - maybe that's just me though.

By day I was working on a building site and kidding on I knew what I was doing and I wasn't the only one - as well as my sidekick Lee (since moved to the USA - alright mate) most of the British unemployed of the early nineties must have gone through that site at one point or another. We were building a hotel, a half famous hotel as it happens, that was right on the beach and this was where I spent all of my dinner hours.

Can you imagine a lad from the backstreets of Byker discovering that foreign women were not only a bit smart but also weren't shy about getting their thruppenny bits out - it was like free viagra man. As well as that our crew spent the first two weeks living at the bottom of the famous 'La Rambla', it turned out to be a hotbed of petty crime and prostitution.....and it was brilliant!

I'd never seen a transvestite before and now they were gathering on the street corner where I lived trying to con unwary tourists. I picked up the language quickly and knew enough to get by after the first day; you know the kind of thing - beer, sandwich and fuck you (midre` if you're wondering) before expanding my knowledge and becoming, in my own little way at least, a bit more cosmopolitan.

Then we moved to Castelldefells, a German resort, where we first heard of the 'Olimpic Canale' nightclub, it was basically a collection of open air bars clustered around the man made canal from the '92 Olympics and it was very popular with the locals. The bouncers soon got to know and like us. I think this was mainly because we were English and talked football with them, so we just spent our weekends staggering around the place and trying not to fall into the water without fear of being clouted by unlicensed body builders from the back streets of Barca.

Like I said manna from Nirvana but...I was going to miss a number of matches and that would be hard. News from home wasn't encouraging, we'd done badly in a lot of friendlies (or so it was spun by the media - see nowt changes) and the renowned 'hardman' Neil Ruddock had smashed Peter Beardsley's cheekbone in one of the aforementioned 'friendly' games. Now call me pedantic but if you had just signed for your new club and were anxious to impress a crowd that saw you as the new Tommy Smith wouldn't you decide to make your nasty, cowardly attack on someone a bit bigger than Beardo? Maybe the fact that a certain Scottish chancer with a penchant for 'proper players' (Julian Dicks was another of his signings - Jesus wept) was his new boss had something to do with the unprovoked assault, which had it been on the street would have resulted in arrest, on the nicest most inoffensive man in football - who knows? What it meant to us though was that the main man's return to black and white action had been postponed and we were going into our debut premiership season without our major summer signing.

St. James was full to bursting and the fans that were there were full of optimism and expectancy - after all we'd won our last match by six clear goals and we knew from bitter experience that Ossie's teams couldn't defend. In the event they were brought back down to earth with a thump after a slick moving and experienced Tottenham side took the points through an excellent Sheringham finish. We were second best for most of the match by all accounts as the carnival atmosphere and the occasion of returning to the top division got to the players.

The news filtered through to Spain through a series of phone calls home and the San Miguel didn't taste half as sweet that night and it got worse before it got better as we followed that result with a loss at Coventry - bloody hell man, what was going on? Still it was only Manchester United at Old Trafford next...

We all expected the worst given the doom and gloom we'd been peddled over the phone and read in the British tabloids but the lads showed their mettle and got a creditable draw, Cole netting the equaliser. We followed that with our first win at home to Everton and then a couple of draws. In the meantime it was decided that we would be leaving Spain at the start of September and flying back into Heathrow rather than Newcastle - my first taste of life abroad had come to an end but I'd enjoyed the experience and it fired the wanderlust that still engulfs me today. Luckily my brother was stationed in London then so I got to spend a bit of time with him before we got the bus back to Geordieland in time for me to take in my first match of the season, at home to the Chris Waddle inspired Sheffield Wednesday.

I went to the Stags to meet Col and the lads before the match and was confident of a good reception, particularly as I hadn't mentioned I was coming home. My travelling experience had broadened my horizons immensely and given me new European tastes and attitudes.

'Pint of Scotch pet.'

I caught sight of my deep, three months on a Spanish building site, suntan in the mirror behind the bar and mentally preened myself, I was looking better than Tom Cruise. And so, steeling myself for the emotional outpouring that would doubtless precipitate my re-emergence into Byker society I followed the noise to the pool room and made my entrance.

'Hoo Andy canny tan - you been on holiday?'

'Ya back then Rivs, much action ower there?'

And then the classic, nay immortal, quote, bearing in mind no-one had seen me since May, from one of the more intellectually challenged local boys.

'You weren't out last weekend Andy were you?'

It was good to be back.

The match itself lived up to all of the hype about this team that were becoming known as 'The Entertainers'. We went one up, they equalised and then went ahead through Sinton, a Geordie lad with the good grace not to celebrate his goal too much - unlike a certain ex-winger with mackem tendencies and an aversion to speaking in his proper accent who milked it for all it was worth. As time was running out Keegan introduced Alex Mathie into the fray and we threw everything we had at them. The ball dropped into their eighteen yard area and Cole was there.

Ball - foot - net, two apiece come on.

Then, the moment that I knew we were back, one of those stay with you forever, bore your grandkids with, I was there when it happened, jobs.

The ball was knocked long from the back over Mathie's head, he chased it followed by a defender, seemed to slip but threw his leg at it anyway and the ball dinked perfectly over the keeper's head at speed. It looked an amazing goal in the ground and even better on the telly that night when I got home, some pundits tried to claim it was a fluke but Mathie said he meant it and I believed him.

I still do.

Malcolm Allen, an excellent but unlucky bargain buy finished them off with number four and we were done. The seeds of the nation's second favourite team had been sown and I had finally witnessed my team back in the big league. In the words of the locals from my now second favourite city - 'Muy Bien Jordee.'

Eurodizzy 93-94

In the summer of '94 I got itchy feet again, the bits of work I was doing here and there had dried up, the football season was over for a while at least and I was sick of being skint. So, having been exhorted by Col to 'get a proper fucking job' and with my season ticket renewal bill hanging over me like the grim reaper's scythe must surely hang over John McCriricks clotted arteries, I resolved to redouble my efforts and put in a shift at the Jobcentre every day.

Now since I'd come back from Barcelona I'd really got the taste for working abroad and broadening my horizons but there wasn't any work for an unskilled toe rag like my good self, even one as good at blagging it as I now undoubtedly was. Until, one day I saw this advert for Coach Hosts to travel with holidaymakers to their destinations - sounded great. I told everyone I was going to be a rep and they were jealous as anything until I explained it would be on a bus for three days at a time between Geordieland and Northern Spain, they weren't that bothered then.

Still host or rep sounded better than unemployed and I did get a freebie holiday thrown in at some point, wages were rubbish but I reckoned there'd be bound to be a way I could improve them somewhere along the line. The only fly in the ointment was that for the duration of the contract I'd be overlapping the start of the season and missing our first sortie into Europe since I was knee high to a pitbull.

Thinking that I'd get around it when it happened I applied for the job and, as I'm a people person, got an interview. Now these were being held down near Manchester and I'd claimed to be able to speak conversational Spanish on the application so, as I was very rusty by now, a bit of creative planning was called for. I'd enlisted the help of my neighbour Vic for a lift down there and bought a teach yourself tape for the journey - which he was obviously thrilled about.

By the time we got there I sounded like a trainee Julio Geordio but reckoned I'd get away with it. During the interview I mentioned Spain three times but they never asked me once about my second language (second language? - I can only just manage English) I didn't think it was worth mentioning this to Vic as, after the journey down there, I figured it might send him over the edge. Anyway, I passed the interview then tolerated my three-day induction; again down by Manchester, with my fellow new recruits, the majority of whom wouldn't have looked out of place protesting on a bypass with Swampy and his mates. I'm not a snobbish type of lad but I wouldn't have bought the big issue off some of this mob let alone the unique, rich and satisfying coffee blend specially designed for my new, budget travel, employer and their discerning clientele.

So, no sooner was I officially on the team than I received my first call to go down South and pick up the returning Newcastle coach. Twelve hours later I'm standing on Dover docks waiting for the coach, bricking it and frantically going over all of my training (three whole days! Professional outfit this like). Sell coffee, do headcount, sell coffee, read script over microphone, sell coffee, chat to passengers and ask about their holidays, sell coffee, put videos on and devise amusing quizzes to pass the time, sell coffee.

Then it came and all I could think was - how do I look? Suit on, hair brushed, shoes polished, must remember I'm the customer's image of the company. I spent the whole eight hours on the bus down here going over my hundred and fifty page hand book and I'm ready, No I'm not, the coach is pulling up and my mind's just gone blank - Shite.

As the doors opened the two drivers were waiting for me - Kevin and Ivor, they must have been going on fifty but were a right pair of lads. My suspicions about these two were confirmed thirty seconds later when they told me 'Don't bother with a headcount son they're all on, just raffle this case of lager by the time we get to Milton Keynes and we'll split the money.'

Oh yes. From that point on I knew I was going to like these boys.

So my summer went on like that for a bit, I made some cash, renewed my season ticket and was still in The Stags with the lads for four nights out of the seven every week - excellent.

Then the football season started and we went off like a train, Keegan had bought the likes of Hottiger and Albert. He'd moved Venison into midfield and it was paying dividends, we won nine out of our first eleven matches in all competitions and looked the business. All the while this was going on I would spend three days a week on the coaches and enjoy every minute of it. The banter combined with the money making opportunities was something else and, while on every coach I had someone who resented the fact that they had to be there and wanted to take it out on me, I was revelling in the fact that I wasn't actually touching my wages and for once had a healthy bank account. A typical journey for me would start early and be something like this - picture the scene:-

Newcastle Bus station at four in the morning, get passengers checked on and sat down, sell coffee, turn lights on low, bit of spiel on mike, check no-one else wants coffee and off we go to Sunderland (its alright I've had a tetanus). At first I was confused as to how I was going to eat for three days but Kev the driver soon put me straight, all of the service stations give drivers free meals as long as they're in uniform and come in with a load of passengers. As I was in uniform and always came in with a coachload of disorientated bodies the staff assumed I was a driver and treated me accordingly, obviously I felt bad about conning them like that, well for the few seconds before my first free meal anyway. I was soon eating very well indeed. While the general public were paying a fiver for a bit of toast I was getting steak and chips everywhere for nowt. I thought getting free tapes and stuff through my new Granada loyalty card was kicking the arse out of it a bit but hey, if you don't ask you don't get.

At Dover the coaches from around the country lined up together and were allocated resort destinations, the first time

I went I was given a place in Northern Spain, Tossa Del Mar (pretty apt some might say) and a whole new set of passengers/problems/financial opportunities.

You may have worked this out for yourself by now but just in case I'll spell it out for you. My main duty as a coach rep was not to make the passengers life easier or more comfortable but to part them from their money before they got to their resort. This was done by selling them mediocre goods at quality prices with the cash obviously all going back to the company. However, as a firm believer in the free market I'd spend all of the night before a trip carefully spooning decent coffee into the plastic cups I'd acquired. I then stuck these at the bottom of my regulation company stacks and at fifty pence a cup I reckoned my intensive beverage dispensing training was going to come in well handy.

Luckily for me as well my first trip into the unknown was on the same coach as Ivor and Kevin. For those of you who don't know, both the driver and the rep are in possession of a microphone to speak to the passengers and as we'd approached Dover I was making my little speech about where to go with passports etc. when they'd intervened and very kindly began to educate me to the ways of the world (well the world of budget coach travel anyway). They told everyone not to bother eating on the ferry as we were going to a proper French village restaurant about fifty kilometres (we're all European now remember) from Calais which was far better value. The passengers all obviously lapped this up and Stena Line didn't make any money that day.

After we'd disembarked and driven for about forty five minutes we got to the restaurant and it was the same drill as in England - a private room and a free meal for drivers and reps - and the lucky holidaymakers got their first taste of being abroad, a long queue and inflated French prices. The hosts and drivers all met up at this place every time going out and coming back so there was a bit of camaraderie amongst us as we compared whinging passengers and our own forms of retribution - remember this was in the days when making a compensation claim was just not a British thing to do and no-one had heard of Oprah Winfrey - so hot coffee over the lap on a bumpy moving coach was simply an accident.

Anyway, I digress, the net result of bringing fifty odd customers into this restaurant was that we would get about fifty quid plus a case of lager and various bits of chocolate. I would then raffle these on the coach and stick another fifty notes into the pot which we'd then split between the three of us. We'd usually hit another place in the South of France for the same deal and always make time to go to the hypermarkets in Calais on the way back (claiming traffic had held us up), where the local hypermarkets fell over themselves to give us money.

So, my trips usually made me about a hundred quid from the pot along with all of my food and drink for free, then I had my coffee money on top so life was good. My reputation was also enhanced amongst the drivers when, being lost in Northern Spain, I had asked a copper the way and understood every word he had said (mind you he spoke English but I kept that to myself).

I'd been 'on the buses' for a month when the payback happened, the toon were making their bow in Europe under Keegan and I'd be in the middle of nowhere and unable to watch it. There was only one thing for it, I'd have to be a big boy, grit my teeth and be nice to people when my mind was obviously elsewhere. We were playing the historic European club of Royal Antwerp over two legs and were away first. When I left the day before the usual 'pundits' and 'experts' had been full of it.

'There's no way Keegan's style of play will work in a European match.'

'They'll have to learn to defend as you simply can't attack freely in these kind of games.'

'It'll be cat and mouse and Newcastle will have to adapt quickly.'

'Newcastle's inexperience will let them down in this game.'

'Newcastle will get fucking hammered.'

Okay I made that last one up but you get the picture.

On the night of the game I was somewhere in France with a coach full of people who didn't give a monkeys if we'd won or not, they were on their way back from their holiday and had to sit on a coach for two days so none of them were what you'd call jovial. Bear in mind as well that this was before mobile phones were being used by anyone other than cockney yuppies and Sky were still allowing the odd game to be played on a Saturday afternoon and you can imagine my frustration (if you can't then you're reading the wrong book).

So I didn't know the score and spent a fitful night worrying. I mean those 'experts' had all played the game hadn't they? They were paid lots of money to be pundits so they must have a good idea of what would happen mustn't they? What is a 'pundit' anyway? It sounds like a cross between arse bandit and a punter, which on some Middlesbrough streets is a good earner by all accounts. Anyway, we got to Calais in the morning and hit the hypermarkets, I didn't even hang around for my bung off the grateful store manager preferring to let the drivers soil their hands for once whilst I went in search of an English paper. Unfortunately I couldn't find one and had to read the Sun but when I did...I was furious.

Furious that I'd wasted a good worry and several minutes of my life listening to the bollocks spouting, cliché ridden spanners that are employed by football shows, newspapers and radio stations. We'd smashed Royal Antwerp five nil...five fucking nil...away from home...in a European game.

We'd scored the first after fifty seconds and it was downhill all the way for the hosts after that. A hatrick from Rob Lee, one from the boy Sellars and a tricky one from the returning Steve Watson saw us shock Europe and made the arse bandit punters on the telly eat their words.

The biggest shock of the night was that Andy Cole hadn't scored but Newcastle United as both a team and a club had made a statement to the world of football- we really were back - and it didn't end there either. The toon continued to play well in the league and I caught the return game against Antwerp when we battered them again by a score of five goals to two. In retrospect, maybe this game should have given us cause for concern, we were four nil up (nine nil on aggregate) and started arsing about which resulted in them scoring two quick ones before Andy, Andy Cole got the ball and scored another goal. Now everyone was jubilant on the night but that mini collapse and subsequent fifth goal for us only served to mask failings that would cost us dear in the next round.

Coachwise life went on and so did I but it couldn't last, after a little while I started to fall foul of my employers, they obviously realised I was having a good time and weren't having that. I knew it couldn't be my work as we had to give out comments forms for people to fill in on their way home and apart from a couple of carefully selected mediocre ones in the interests of balance, any that were less than complimentary about me never got past the bin, apart from one which we shall discuss later - most people liked me anyway, honest. My coaches started to get inspected regularly by the auditors, they'd caught a couple of people out by finding jars of coffee hidden in their bags or extra money in their float. They could never catch me though as even though it has been said in the past that I'm a lazy sod (I prefer lethargic - it's all to do with my low blood pressure), I'm very, very efficient where my money is concerned.

As I said before, I used to spend hours in the house before I went on a trip spooning coffee into little cups with powdered milk, I would then add these cups to the bottom of the company pile and sell them at a fifty-fifty split from the top and bottom of the stack. My float would always be spot on as my money would go straight into my pocket and their money straight in the bag, what they also didn't know was that the drivers kept in touch with each other and as soon as an auditor or supervisor was spotted the word would be around every coach.

So I knew I was being kept an eye on but as well as being quite a confident young man I've always taken the advice from the George Orwell book 'Nineteen Eighty Four', you can get away with anything if you keep the little rules and break the big ones, sound advice I've always thought. In summary, I was clean-shaven, sober, polite, organised and could talk for hours about anything but I was also robbing the company blind and letting passengers drink their raffled lager on the coach.

On my return to Newcastle I took stock of my financial position and came to the decision that as the season wouldn't go on forever I really needed to be maximising my earnings. I didn't fancy doing the ski resorts and given my propensity for cheek and general piss taking of all things in authority I didn't think I'd be invited back next year. Thinking logically though how hard could it be? I had a captive audience for three days, they obviously had money, they were uncomfortable, tired and missing their normal surroundings - should be easy. I just needed to be inventive, creative and above all cheap - everyone else was knocking cans of pop out at sixty pence so I sold mine at fifty pence, I was buying and selling a box of tobacco every week and Kwiksave couldn't keep up with my demand for coffee.

Life was good and I was in my own private utopia, making a very comfortable living for not much work therefore it was inevitable that it had to end prematurely and end it did. Oh and if you were in the crowd at St. James Park on the eighteenth of October that year then it was probably your bloody fault. Mind you, in all fairness, the holiday season was virtually over anyway and the way I got caught out was comical. That night was when we played Athletic Bilbao at home in the next round of the UEFA Cup. We went three nil up, playing the brand of football that was now our trademark, through Fox, Beardsley and Cole. In the final twenty minutes the crowd started a Mexican wave, the team relaxed thinking it was over and Bilbao got two very important goals. They were to prove crucial in the return leg, the home team beating us one nil and going through on away goals. Keegan himself attributed the teams collapse to the start of the dreaded 'wave' at St. James.

And why did I get sacked because of it I hear you ask? Well I'd gone to my mates flat to watch the match and taken my latest batch of comments forms for 'selective disposal', a few cans later and shredded nerves brought on by what I knew was now going to be a hard away leg and my thinking wasn't as straight as it should have been - I let one go that I should have binned straight off. The one that caught me out was positively glowing in its praise of me, so much so that I didn't read it all properly. The person commented that he only had one tongue in cheek complaint and that was to do with the firms catering and as that was nothing to do with me I didn't read it all. To be honest, after the event, I could see the chap's point of view, when you've paid a pound for a hot dog you expect it to be hot, the company agreed and gave him a ring asking how he'd acquired it on a coach without a kitchen?

The gentleman eager to help the friendly Geordie coach host with whom he'd shared a couple of laughs told them that I'd used the water from the kettle and sold them to everyone and that they were on the whole very nice.

So come the next day Kevin Keegan, the whole Newcastle United squad and myself had one thing in common - we were all out of Europe.

<u>Man Utd (h) 94-95</u>

By the time Christmas '94 was approaching my life had reached a dead end. My last job had been on the coaches and the money from that was gone leaving me surviving on whatever the state gave me. I hated not working and worse still, could feel the apathy setting in as I started to struggle to get out of bed in the morning. When I did have money I would undoubtedly blow it on going out and would often spend the whole week getting over what I'd got up to at the weekend.

Things had to change the question was how?

My saviour was my mate Rob, in the Stags he mentioned to me that he was moving South to a place called Banbury for work and asked if I'd be interested in coming with him. I weighed up my options. The rest of my life on the dole and a growing sense of underachievement and missed opportunity fermenting into sourness at a wasted life or a step into the unknown and a chance of a new existence.

I started packing when I got home.

I said my goodbyes two weeks before Christmas and the lads took it with a pinch of salt. After all I fucked off every other week it seemed to them, but I meant to make something of myself and the poxy jobs I'd took in the past like selling sandwiches from a van or washing traffic cones in the rain weren't going to do that. I arrived in Banbury on a wet Friday morning determined to have a go at carving something out for myself, my lift was packed with food parcels from me mam who, quite rightly, realised how fucking useless I was. I couldn't say I'd ever really heard of the place but it seemed alright, a quaint market town with loads of pubs - that'll do for me.

I started work immediately, doing a shift that very night, and was soon temping around the many warehouses that populated the place. The coldness of my bedsit kept out by the warm feeling having money in my pocket gave me.

We had a rubbish Christmas down there that year but there was too much work on to go home and I was determined not to give up. My brother Darrell and cousin Paul came to visit for New Years Eve, they turned up in a German car that our Daz had driven all the way from his base in Deutschland and apparently it kept cutting out on the motorway and was a bit of a deathtrap...so he gave it to me for Christmas...well, after he'd taken a hammer to the dashboard to get the radio out anyway.

That was me mobile and able to get to the warehouses and factories on the edge of town under my own steam, as long as when I was on morning shifts I was able to scrape the ice from the inside of the windscreen and work the manual choke anyway (I kept the windows shut to avoid the smoke...). Once the festivities were over they were offski and I turned my attention back to the serious business of earning a crust, believe me I worked everywhere; from a chocolate factory to a computer games warehouse.

Then as I was thinking of making a trip home to use my mainly redundant season ticket Keegan dropped a bombshell, he sold Andy Cole to Man Utd. Our next game? You've guessed it at home to the Red Devils - now I was definitely going. We got a massive fee at the time for Cole, six million of the finest English notes plus Keith Gillespie, and even now with the benefit of hindsight I think we got the best of the deal. Cole was a one trick pony at Newcastle and teams had sussed us out, Keegan made a brave, but ultimately correct, decision and it benefited the team in the long run.

The train up to Newcastle then cost fifty quid return and the car wasn't reliable enough to travel more than a couple of miles, add in the fact that it was playing up every day and if I wanted to keep it I'd have to convert it from left hand drive and it's fate was sealed. As the scrapman hoisted it onto the back of his lorry and I put the cash he'd given me into my back pocket I swear the headlight gave me a little wink as I said goodbye - mind you it was early Saturday morning so that might have been the lager from the night before.

Coming back over the river on the train was magnificent. I've heard people say before that when you see the Tyne Bridge it chokes you up and I'd never really understood it until that moment. Something hit me hard in the chest, round about where my heart should be, and made me gasp as my town came into view. I could even see the Byker Wall away in the distance and finally understood why people called it Legoland (fuck off man it's won awards you know). I hadn't been gone that long yet it felt like a million years and as I alighted at Central Station I felt like a prodigal son - even better though, I knew me mam would feed me right up - get in.

When Keegan had sold Cole some people had reacted badly, they'd accused the club of thinking in the short term and cashing in on our best players just like in previous era's at St. James. They were wrong. This was a new club with a new outlook and Kevin took the unprecedented step of coming out at the main entrance to the ground and explaining his reasoning to them. I was worried that the bad feeling would spill over at the match but had no need to be. Cole and Gillespie had been left out of both teams by mutual agreement and the atmosphere was electric, the travelling Man Utd fans started singing the Andy Cole song to taunt us but were simply met with an wall of noise in support of Kevin Keegan. It wasn't a classic game but we got a one all draw and left the ground reasonably happy.

In the Stags after that came a moment that tested my resolve to carry on with my new life and an opportunity for me to slip back into the existence I had worked so hard to change. I had agreed to sell my season ticket as I couldn't afford to keep travelling back on the train and the lad was a little bit late for our tradeoff.

I could just slip over the road to me mam's, plonk myself on the settee and sign back on at the DSS on Monday. Easy.

Ten minutes later, having made the right decision for once, I was handing the ticket over. I thought that was hard but getting on the train the next day, hungover and sad, beat that easily. I waved at my bridge as I travelled in the opposite direction this time and hoped I was doing the right thing.

Back in my tiny, cold bedsit that night I put on some tunes and took stock of what I'd come back to. As the Inspiral Carpets filled the air I looked at the space where the telly should be, glanced at the damp climbing up the walls and pressed the emergency credit button on the electric meter to ensure I could at least listen to my stereo for a little bit longer.

'No-one ever said it was gonna be easy...'

Fucking right there mate.

Aston Villa (a) 97-98

I'd lived in Banbury a couple of years by now and had spent fortunes travelling to Newcastle every other week for the match and was looking for a way to cut costs. In one of my regular strokes of genius I had realised that, while it was the middle of nowhere football wise it was also the middle of everywhere geographically. I also, it transpired, knew a few Villa lads down here and following Keegan's shock resignation they were travelling up to Birmingham for the forthcoming Newcastle match. It was a bit late for me to get tickets for the toon end but the Villa lads sorted me out a ticket in the Doug Ellis Stand with the disclaimer - 'You'll be alright, it's all families in there but keep your mouth shut....'

I met them at the train station, we had a few cans on the train and a bit of a crack before getting into Birmingham, as I'd never been there before and I knew it was a big city I'd naively assumed it'd be like the toon - not so. Where I thought there'd be loads of claret and blue shirted gadgies milling around and singing there were shoppers, where I'd envisaged lads flogging fanzines and old programme vendors there were Big Issue sellers and where I'd expected to hear drunken banter and clinking glasses there was polite conversation (albeit in a fucking ridiculous accent) and people eating their dinner - Jesus so this is what Mars was like?

We hit a boozer in the city centre and had a couple of bevvies whereupon I realised the reason for the lack of big match atmosphere, Villa Park was actually miles away from the centre. As I mentioned, Birmingham is a big city and unlike the toon where St. James sits proudly looking over the whole place Villa Park is actually some distance out of town in a place called, funnily enough, Aston. Anyway, after mocking their town for a while the lads obviously decided to teach me a lesson and we moved on to a place just outside the ground. It was a run down, seedy looking drinking den with no windows called 'The Upper Grounds' and it was members only. Well, I say members only, if the bouncer didn't recognise you (and it must have been hard for him having only the one eye) then you had to be with a face he did know and also pay a quid for the liberty of him having to do his job. Anyway, it was sorted and I was in. The place was a hooligan wannabe's wet dream, Burberry had obviously despatched their top salesman to Aston going by the amount of 'geezer' wear in evidence. It was my round but one of my companions physically stopped me from going to the bar and whispered to keep a low profile in here - obviously thinking I was stupid enough to order a bottle of dog and start singing Blaydon Races. We had a couple of pints and I listened to the banter in the bar, mainly regarding Keegan and I was dying to retaliate a bit but I kept a lid on it. The lads' uncle walked in with one of their cousins and we were introduced, with them being told to keep it down about my Geordieness, and more pints were had then we set off for the match.

We sorted out a post match meeting point before I was deposited at my turnstile and they headed for the Holte End, so this was it, behind enemy lines, luckily I wasn't scared.

Unluckily I was pissed.

Following Kev's departure Terry Mac and Arthur Cox had taken over team affairs for this match and it was pretty much as you were. The Villa fans were obviously vocal about our messiah leaving and the massed ranks of Geordies were equally as defiant in the away end. It was strange for me to be in the middle of them both and while I knew I was inebriated this also added to my feelings of disorientation, I should have been in there with the 'Northern Bastards.' The teams came out and the familiar, gut churning feeling started, the pride in my city started rising from deep inside towards my mouth and I knew I wouldn't be able to hold it in for ninety minutes. In the event I couldn't even hold it in for the whole sixteen minutes it took us to score. Shearer chased down a lost cause, shoulder charged an obviously soft defender out of the way and lashed the ball straight into the back of the net.

Cue wild celebrations in the away end, massive Shearer directed recriminations all round the ground and me? Well, I held it in for ...ooh microseconds before I jumped up and let everyone know just who I was and where I was from. To be fair to the shocked Brummies all around me they were quite lenient, only gobbing on me and shouting abuse rather than any kind of physical assault.

Then, five whole minutes later, we scored again,

Bosnich went to welly it down the pitch and Shearer 'allegedly' grasped at one of his legs from the floor where he'd been knocked down, the keeper scuffed it straight to Lee Clark who promptly volleyed it straight back over him. That was me back on my feet as obviously they all claimed it was a foul and I pointed out it was a mans game and they were 'soft southern bastards'. Even through my pissed up state I was hoping the stewards would move me to the safety of the toon end but all I got was more hockle and the odd shove. Fuck them, we were winning two-nil and the defiant chorus 'Newcastle UNITED will never be defeated' was echoing across Villa Park - it was great. Obviously being Newcastle it couldn't, and didn't last, they got one back and all around me Brummies pointed, gesticulated and generally let me know that they were back in it.

'Bollocks,' I said, 'we're still winning.'

Then they scored again. Fucking delirium in the Doug Ellis Stand and, as I sat slumped in my seat, the odd cuff round the head from a mob handed brummie. Again, fuck them, we weren't losing. It was an uneasy standoff for the rest of the game, if the toon had scored I was obliged to celebrate after my previous outbursts but I would almost certainly have been kicked to bits, on the other hand, fuck it, I didn't want the toon to lose just to save my own skin - that just went against the grain. The minutes ticked on and I was considering loudly proclaiming that I was off to the toilet before doing a runner when it happened...Villa got a penalty. They were all jumping around me again, laughing, pointing, gobbing, cuffing and shoving. I couldn't fuck off now, it would be admitting defeat, I would have to endure the rest of the match and take the consequences at the end. So I sat stoic and unbowed as they sang Dwight Yorke's name as he placed the ball. I prepared myself for the abuse as he ran...then I exploded out of my seat as he missed and serenaded the entire Doug Ellis stand with 'What the fucking hell was that HA HA' .....and ran for my life.

Later on, having successfully negotiated meeting my two mates without losing my teeth, I was back in The Upper Grounds having a pint while the train station calmed down. Then their uncle, whom I'd met previously, came wandering back in, he caught sight of me and strode over proclaiming loudly 'Geordie, I've always liked Shearer but he was a fucking cheat today.'

Apparently heads turned, glasses were dropped and pool cues brandished after that...I couldn't say for certain as before he got to the end of his sentence I was two miles away in a taxi looking for New Street Station. It was a baptism of fire for my debut appearance in Brummieland but well worth it as Villa Park, to me anyway, is a proper old school football ground with a history to match ours.

Mind you ever since then I've made sure that I get a ticket for the away end when we play there.

A Tale of two finals 98-99

On the Sixteenth of May 1998 Newcastle United walked out at Wembley for the FA Cup Final against Arsenal. It was my first one since '76 when I'd been far too young to have any idea of what it meant. Back then it wasn't really the end of the world as we'd been in a final only two years previously when a Kevin Keegan inspired Liverpool had twatted us without really trying. So to my young mind this kind of thing happened all the time and it was obvious we'd win a cup any day now.

Fast forward twenty two years and I was getting a bit desperate but this was our big chance. You see the omens were good, forget the fact that Arsenal were the Premiership champions and head and shoulders above everyone else, forget the fact we had finished thirteenth in the league with football so boring and depressing that Jack Charlton would have been embarrassed (mind you, wait until Souness turned up). Forget all that, I knew we would win because I'd left my job in the previous January and as part of my leaving present I'd been presented with a ten pound bet on Newcastle to win the FA Cup at odds of fifteen to one - I knew we were going to win because of this fact alone.

In the event I wasn't so much clutching at straws as grabbing big fistfuls straight out of a barn but you always have to have a reason to be positive don't you and, hey man, this was the Cup Final.

JESUS CHRIST MAN WE'RE IN THE FA CUP FINAL...

I had no chance of a ticket for the match itself so made plans to be back in the toon for the bars opening at eleven. I had to work nightshift doing a stocktake on the Friday so went straight from work to the train station. I was on the train at about half six, had my first can at twenty five to seven and was singing along to the Charlatans on my disc player (remember them? Thank god for mp3's) by quarter to the hour. Luckily for my neighbours on the carriage I was spark out by eight o clock and they didn't hear another peep out of me until Durham.

I met Col and our Paul and we headed for the Bigg Market, confident of a victory after I had relayed my news of the lucky bet. A few naysayers told me to lay it off - were they mental? Dilute my winnings just because they had no faith - I kept it tight in my pocket and mentally spent the money on drink as the lads took to the field.

I should have known. The Arsenal team consisted of the likes of Anelka, Overmars, Viera and Petit. They also had the renowned back four of Adams, Keown, Dixon and Winterburn. In return we could offer up an increasingly immobile Shearer and a flairless, functional team that relied heavily on an ageing Robert Lee. Dalglish also seemed to have played Barton the right side of midfield with the left back, Pistone, behind him. This was presumably to counter the speed and skill of their left winger by doubling up on him and using Pistone's own pace to good effect. The tactic was obviously to sit back, keep it tight and hope for the best. This has been similarly employed by a succession of managers since (Souness, Allardyce and Kinnear spring to mind) and with about as much success as it got us on this day.

We allowed Arsenal to dictate the game and they quickly took control scoring in the twenty third minute through guess who? Yup, Marc Overmars simply ignored Kenny's clever attempt to stifle him and ran faster than both Pistone and Barton before slotting home. We had a bit of a go and Dabizas hit the crossbar before the turning point of the match.

I was in a boozer at the top of the Bigg Market directly in front of a big screen and had a brilliant view of what occurred. Martin Keown slipped and Shearer, denied any kind of service from Dalglish's team of defenders, was on it. He placed a shot expertly past Seaman's despairing dive and we rose as one in the bar, coming back down just in time to see it rebound back off the post and out to safety. I knew then and so did everyone else, we'd be waiting a bit longer for the first trophy of my entire lifetime and I'd be drinking my own money that night instead of the bookies.

Anelka, sportingly finished us off not long later instead of allowing us to agonisingly hope and that was it. I was mortal down the Bigg Market for about an hour after the match and didn't see any of the supposed violence or damage - in fact I was bloody surprised when I read about it the next day - I heard only supportive chanting from the longest suffering fans in world football.

Our support at Wembley had been magnificent and our team, and primarily our manager, had been spineless. This was the first time I'd heard the 'attack, attack, attack' chant but it wouldn't be the last and the fallout from this sorry showing manifested itself in Dalglish's departure at the start of the next season. Shepherd showing superb timing as ever in allowing Kenny to blow the transfer budget before sacking him and bringing in Mad Ruud.

Amazingly we somehow got to Wembley again the very next season. I feel that was despite Mr. Gullit rather than because of him incidentally, and guess what? You've got it - we played the champions (soon to be treble winners) again.

This time I didn't have the lucky omen of a bet and I pretty much knew we'd lose again, but fuck it, I stored up the brownie points with our lass and took my place on the daft o clock train to Newcastle on Cup Final day 99'.

Unfortunately for my neighbours on the overpriced, clanking old heap of shit this time I hadn't been up all night and was wide awake and determined to enjoy my day. They got Oasis, the Stone Roses and the Mondays whilst I got slowly pissed, cleverly drowning out the agony of getting so near yet so far again. We watched this one in the Middle Club in Byker on the big screen, hoping not so much for a win but just a performance to be proud of, hoping we'd at least have a go this time. It was not to be.

We briefly had reason for optimism when Gary Speed clouted 'hard man' Roy Keane and he had to go off but it was all downhill from there.

Looking back at it now their front two of Cole and Solskaer, bolstered by the arrival of Teddy Sheringham when Keane went off, were never going to lose much sleep over the combined central defensive talents of Dabizas and Charvet. We had chances when Ketsbaia hit the post and Maric dragged it wide when one on one with Schmeichel but in the main they outclassed us from start to finish and it could have been a lot worse. Giggs, Beckham and Cole should all have scored, Sheringham should have had a hatrick but only got the one, Solskaer had one cleared off the line, Paul Scholes got his usual goal against us and we were humiliated at Wembley again.

There was no disgrace in losing to the eventual treble winners (they were a fucking good team after all - still are in fact) but another spineless display left the fans more frustrated than ever.

Me? I just drank to forget - I still can't though, our kid won't let me.

LET'S PUSH THINGS FORWARD

The Noughties

Local Hero

The start of the following season saw us all in confident mood. Our cup final exploits for the second year in a row, combined with some astute looking transfers, had us all dreaming of great things again as we skipped up death alley to our spiritual home. Gullit had obviously recognised our deficiencies and acted accordingly bringing in three highly rated defenders, Goma, Marcelino and the vastly experienced Dumas. He'd supplemented this by acquiring the exciting young talent of Kieron Dyer to complement our twin destroyers up front, Shearer and Ferguson. Things were looking good.

As the teams came out for the start of the first game versus Villa I mentioned to my neighbour in the East Stand (yeah I was getting to that age...) that we could well do something this season and he agreed as did most of the city judging by the people I spoke to. Unfortunately, what we all failed to realise however was that as Newcastle United supporters we are obliged to be disappointed every year, with the only variable being just what month our season ends. In recent campaigns it's been sometime around Christmas.

Anyway, we were all in buoyant mood as the game kicked off and I noted that the referee was that one who did the karate 'wouldn't like to get on the wrong side of him' I thought. Unfortunately Shearer did upset him by blatantly and maliciously breathing, so Uriah Rennie had no choice but to send him off, much to the amazement of Villa's Ian Taylor. Rennie then continued to harass and harangue Shearer for the rest of his playing career in an effort to make a name for himself. Incidentally Uriah if you're reading this I've got a name for you and it starts with a C.

We lost the game one-nil and it was the beginning of the end for Ruud. His decisions became increasingly more erratic and panic stricken, culminating in leaving out a fit pairing of Ferguson and Shearer in favour of a young reserve named Robinson (no not that one) for the crunch match against the mackems. We all know what happened that night, how it lashed down and they used the conditions to bring us down to their level before fluking two goals but, even though they were lucky, we'd still been beaten by our nearest rivals and Ruud was out. There was speculation that he'd wanted to go, that the job was too much for him and the press interest too intrusive. If that was the case then the team he picked against Sunderland, which was described at the time as 'the best resignation note in football', certainly did the trick. We needed a new manager, a proper one, a manager without gimmicks or still wet behind the ears, someone who had been there, seen it and bought the tee-shirt.

On the second of September in the year of our lord nineteen ninety nine Bobby Robson, world renowned football manager and a Geordie born and bred came home. His first game in charge was away to Chelsea some two days later and we all expected the worst. In the event we lost one nil to a penalty that should never have been and, while not causing them too many problems, we looked solid and hard to break down - the revolution had started.

With my usual brilliant timing I went on holiday to Lefkas in Greece before our next game. This was away to CSKA Sofia in Bulgaria and as usual the pundits had us beat before we started. Mooching along the main street in the resort I listened through the open doors of the bars for the sounds of an English commentator and, just as I was coming to terms with the awfulness of not watching the lads, I heard the word 'Robson' and I dragged my wife, who doesn't like football much, into the bar quicker than Pete Doherty could dispose of the contents of a packet of Lemsip(I'm speaking metaphorically like). Obviously she was thrilled.

I lined up the bottles of Mythos and settled myself in, thinking this would be a tough one but in actual fact it wasn't that hard. It was a scrappy, kick everything that moves, kind of game at first but we tried to play football, got it down, passed and moved and had a go. It had nil-nil written all over it, which given our recent form, wouldn't have been a bad result. Then in the fifty first minute we got a free kick outside their box about twenty five yards out and Solano shaped up to take it. It was a fucking peach - well actually it was a goal but you know what I mean - the ball flew into the top corner and their keeper got nowhere near it. I jumped (as you do) when the ball hit the back of the net and quickly worked out in mid shout that I was the only one cheering. Our lass, bless her, realised that as well so she joined in to give me moral support whilst the whole bar full of slack jawed dullards that had hoped we'd get beat just stared at us. The things you do for love eh pet?

They came at us repeatedly, as you'd expect the home team to do and we soaked it up and counter attacked when possible. In the seventy sixth minute we only scored again, Temuri Kestbaia doing what he does best and being a little twisty, turny, mad thing and that was that. Bobby's, indeed the club's, first win of the season and it set us up nicely for the cruncher coming up on the Sunday. Sheffield Wednesday, the only team below us in the league were coming to St. James Park for what, even at this early stage in the season, was a six pointer. This would be a stern test of Robson's credentials after all his time away from English football and would probably tell us all that we needed to know about our new manager. Fuck me did it.

I was still in Lefkas and our lass had declined my kind offer of sitting in front of Sky Sports News in a bar on the Sunday afternoon in favour of staying on the beach (lasses eh? Mental man). So I passed the time with a bit of inter club banter between fellow members of the 'can't lie on the sand when my team are playing' brigade and hoped Jeff Stelling would be kind. I needn't have worried, the bar room chat about Shearer being 'past it' and us going down was stopped early on in the match as Hartlepool Jeff reported that Aaron Hughes had scored for us. I went for another pint as I'd made a deal that I'd make my pints last between goals, I'd even went as far as to say that I'd only count Newcastle goals, big of me eh - and with hindsight rather clever.

The goals never stopped after that as Sheff Wed shamefully gave up and as we all know Shearer got five, the team scored eight and Bobby was off and running. Relegation was a distant memory from that game on but more importantly our performance had stopped the abuse from the neutrals in the bar as some of them got genuinely worried we were about to become a force again.

By the time our lass came to get me I was a gibbering wreck and she, reasoning that if you can't beat them etcetera, joined in the spirit of things. When I woke up the next morning I could have sworn that the beer monkey that had plagued me occasionally (well regularly really) during my supporting life, had nicked all my cash, punched me repeatedly in the head and then shit in my mouth before nicking the aspirins. But, as the memories of yesterdays game filtered through my lager damaged brain I realised that in the grand scheme of things my bad head simply didn't matter.

Newcastle were back ...again.

Wemberlee, Wemberlee 99-00

Amazingly, given that we'd been at Wembley for the last two Cup Finals and our team had been allowed to deteriorate under the stewardship of both Dalglish and Gullit we got there again this season.

This time it was a semi-final against Chelsea, but the FA (along with every bloody government since I've been alive) not realising that some people in the country live outside of London decided to hold both of the matches at Wembley. Interestingly here's a little fact for you that most people won't know. As a result of the decision to play the match here it meant that Newcastle United never lost an FA Cup tie outside of Wembley for over three years. Impress your mates down the boozer with that one.

I didn't travel back to the toon for this one as I'd been up the week before for the home match against Bradford and didn't have the cash. I was confident we'd get to the Final anyway and as the other semi consisted of Aston Villa and Bolton Wanderers, neither of whom were world beaters, I knew, I just knew, that if we got through we'd win the Cup. It all hinged on another Wembley occasion and whether we'd actually turn up this time. We had thirty four thousand fans inside Wembley and as usual the place was a sea of black and white. The atmosphere was something to behold and for once the team didn't let us down. The only thing we were lacking on this occasion was luck.

Lee and Speed controlled the middle of the park, Dyer and Solano caused havoc down the flanks and we created numerous chances, unfortunately they weren't falling to Shearer though and we wasted opportunities. Chelsea had in their ranks one of the less heralded, yet excellent, foreign imports to the Premier League. Gustavo Poyet, a Uruguayan with a taste for scoring important goals, particularly against us, filled his boots again. He scored the first for Chelsea against the run of play but we kept going and were outstanding for long periods of the game. We equalised with the first goal I'd ever seen us score at Wembley. Shearer got the ball on the right wing and Lebouef, who always shit himself when faced with the sheet metal workers son, sold himself short as Big Al feinted to go one way then went another. Shearer had often proclaimed himself the best crosser of the ball at the club and the one he whipped over into the box bore out that claim. It was met by Robert Lee, a player who had been an outcast at the start of the season prior to Robson's arrival, and he powered it into the net past a helpless keeper. This was truly game on.

Then I made my fatal mistake, I went to the bog as Dyer got fouled, he went down and stayed down. I assumed the ref would stop the game for treatment before we took our free kick so reckoned I had a couple of minutes grace. I congratulated myself on my good reading of the game as I heard no shouts whilst in the little boy's room but upon exiting I glanced at a screen and felt pain rise up through my body like ink up blotting paper. The cockney bastards had only scored when we were down to ten men, the ref hadn't even given us a free kick and they'd kept the ball rather than put it out - wankers.

That blow would have felled lesser teams, it would certainly have seen the teams managed by Dalglish and Gullit put up the white flag, but not Robson's boys they simply redoubled their efforts. Dyer and Solano both went close and De Goey, in the Chelsea goal, made two brilliant saves to deny us near the end. When the whistle went we were frustrated but proud, sad but not embarrassed. Gianluca Vialli, the Chelsea boss said simply 'Newcastle were the better team'.

Bobby Robson commented 'Over the ninety minutes we played as well, if not better, than at any time this season but it wasn't to be our day.' The fans were defiant, London would have been drunk dry that day because we'd at least had a go but I felt that a good chance to put a trophy in the cupboard had passed us by - the curse of Wembley had done us again

Alan Shearer remarked after the match 'The sooner they knock this place down the better for Newcastle United' and frankly, I agreed with every word.

Man Utd (h) 99/00

On my spare room wall I have a picture of Sir Bobby Robson, a couple of other people and my good self, oh Freddy Shepherd's half on there as well but I've managed to crop his porcine features thus improving the overall effect. Next to the picture I have a framed Newcastle Shirt signed by all the players on the day of this match. It obviously has pride of place on my wall and has a little story behind it (don't they all).

One of my mates, who shall remain nameless, actually no let's give him a name. Let's call him Luke after Paul Newman in the film about the bloke with the cool hand who ate all the eggs (you know who you are - and you'd better have bloody paid for this book as well!)

My mate Luke, rang me on a Monday and asked if I was planning to go to the upcoming home match against the mighty red devils (obviously he didn't call them that - I'm just paraphrasing in preference to recording the string of expletives I'd have to use if I repeated what he really said). I replied in the negative as I didn't have a ticket and fifty quid on petrol is a lot on the offchance I might get one. Fear not, said he (again I'm paraphrasing - this bloke's from Burradon not Brideshead) I've acquired two VIP tickets, free bar, three course meal and a seat in the directors box and you can have one. Obviously there's always a catch where good fortune like this is concerned but this wasn't such a big one - he simply wanted driving up to the toon for nowt and given that I'd probably drink my own weight in free booze this wasn't the end of my world.

So with the bartering completed and times and locations agreed I got on with my week.

*****

We met on the Friday night at the agreed time, set off and as we did so I noticed he had a brand new Newcastle away top still in the sports shop carrier bag. He confirmed that he'd bought it that day and then with a wink and a tap of the side of his nose said why.

'Our sis's gadgy's mam works in them function rooms at the ground - she'll get it signed for us man. I can flog it then.'

I admired his cheek and then got on with the business of driving, a task that got decidedly harder as we hit Catterick and everything ground to a halt. There'd been an accident that scuppered our chances of getting there early enough to go out - never mind it would just make us thirstier the next day. Mind you, if the government decreed that us Northern types were useful for anything other than just squeezing for council tax then maybe, just maybe we'd get a proper road with three lanes running into our neck of the woods.

Anyway, I'm digressing. I dropped him off in turnip town and headed to me mams before turning in for the night. I shivered as I passed that Water Board club like.

*****

On match day I met him in the Strawberry for a couple of liveners before we got stuck into the free stuff. I was wearing my best strides and shirt, amazingly he had also dressed correctly for the occasion and after two pints we headed for the main entrance. They let us in with no fuss and we were led to the function room where we'd be getting our meal. As he'd predicted he knew one of the waitresses and handed over the shirt with the immortal line 'It's for a lad I know down in Banbury - we're gonna raffle it off to send him to America' and she fell for it hook, line and sinker not realising the lad was actually him and he fancied a holiday. With the business concluded we set about the main task of the day - drinking - and swiftly got stuck into the lager and whisky chasers before wobbling up to the directors box for the match.

Unfortunately, well for him anyway, Tim Healy happened to walk around the corner before we got up the steps and was accosted by my mate with the immortal line 'Hoo Tim, how's your lass - still pulling pints in the Rovers?' Mr Healy, being one of the lads and obviously recognising that there'd been some alcohol consumption gone on, took this in good heart and posed for pictures before moving on and we headed up the steps to the promised land.

Now I'd been in the director's box once before but that was back in the early nineties and things had changed. This was brilliant, dead centre of the pitch and surrounded by people I recognised. Bob Moncur was nearby, Sir Alex Ferguson walked past me (should've took a swing eh? Not the first time he'd have been accosted by a drunk in recent years) and sitting one row down from us was the fairly recently departed Steve Watson. Like a moth to a flame my pissed up partner in crime was drawn to his ginger head shouting 'Hoo Stevie...Stevie man...Stevie, how's it gannin down there?'

Watto, to his credit, turned round, smiled and posed for a photo before settling back in his seat and hoping the piss-head forgot about him for the rest of the match.

To the game itself, well it's fair to say it was a cracker, certainly from our point of view anyway. Duncan Ferguson scored an absolute belter with a turn and volley any Brazilian (particularly Rivelino-ho hum) would have been proud of. Roy Keane got his usual sending off at St. James for being a knob. Andy Cole had his usual goal against us disallowed as the ref said it hadn't crossed the line (it had - HA) and Big Al got a brace and celebrated in his usual fashion to seal a very good three nil win. During this time my mate had got into an argument with a Scottish punter about Duncan Ferguson and Bobby's treatment of him during the game which had threatened to turn violent (I didn't care by this time cos I was mortal) and he'd harassed everyone that had ever thought about being on the local news let alone genuinely famous.

After the match the cool handed one and me celebrated in our usual fashion and necked as much as possible until the bar closed. When it did and they finally persuaded us to leave we happened to be staggering past the boardroom when my pal's itchy camera finger flared up again and he marched in there.

Even in my state I knew that was a bit naughty but I was dumbfounded when he came back out with Freddy Shepherd apparently willing to have his photo taken with us. Now I'm no fan of the man who called me a mug, so I was in two minds as to whether I wanted to be in this picture, but my dithering came to an end two seconds later when Bobby Robson walked around the corner and was dragged into the frame. The result is on my spare room wall for all to see right next to the signed shirt I gave cool hand Luke fifty notes for, but it doesn't quite tell the whole story.

My mate had been a pest all day but in our final drunken moments at St. James and just as the shutter closed on the camera in this the last photo he was given some belated advice by a future knight of the realm.

'You want to calm down son.'

And he immediately did - Bobby had spoken.

Jesus if only I'd known it was that easy two days ago.

Half Time

Clone Island

An introduction to football supporters in the modern age

Having spent the last thirty years watching the lads at grounds up and down this sceptred isle the one thing that I have noticed is this; no matter which part of the country you are in, there are certain types of people who are exactly the same. The accents may sound different and the faces may look dissimilar, but the characteristics remain identical. From Fratton Park all the way up to Gods chosen land you can go into any ground, look around any stand and rest assured that the following selection of supporter types will be present.

The Billy Nee Pals

Billy is easily given away by his propensity to engage everyone from the stewards to the hooligans in inane conversation. The subject matter is not important. What is important to Billy Nee Pals is that he is seen to be on speaking terms with most of the fans, by the rest of the fans. Normally a man, Billy has craved to belong since school. This is where he would always be excluded from joining in with the lads, unless a goalkeeper was needed to make up the numbers for a game of five a side. Billy Nee Pals knows everything about football in general and his team in particular, he will be wearing a big coat covered in badges and patches that denote various times in his teams history. When he's not badgering you to death with his travel tales he'll be boring the tits off you with stories about his new car or teenage girlfriend. After the match Billy then walks home to his mams house and goes straight to his room to read Razzle.

The School Captain

Again, usually a man, the school captain is in his mid-thirties and always turns up in at least one item of football training kit. This lets everyone in the ground know his status as a good player, one who could have turned professional if he didn't injure his *knee/back/little finger. Recently divorced from his wife, who he married at nineteen with the reception, disco and buffet at his football clubhouse. He now realises he isn't a pretty boy any more but can't be bothered to get back in shape to reclaim his past glories so he just wears the gear and slicks his hair back to show off his new diamond earring. The school captain normally stands stock still by his seat and casually reads his programme using it as a cover to check out the lasses scattered around him. He will only venture out to the pie shop at half time if he sees The Hooligans Bird or Match Lass heading that way and he thinks he can impress her.

* Delete as applicable

The Hooligans Bird / Match Lass

The Hooligans Bird and Match Lass are a very different species of female, one (HB) comes to the match wearing full make up, strong perfume and low cut tops. The other (ML) turns up in replica top and trainers, sometimes wearing a humorous wig. As they are different in species the relationship between the two would normally be quite amicable but can become strained and very competitive when HB likes the look of School Captain and ML also thinks she's got a chance. The main difference between the two is their availability. The Hooligans Bird is unattainable mainly due to the surveillance duties of the two big lumps in front of her, whereas the Match Lass is normally accessible and advertises the fact using her two big lumps in front of her.

The Plastic Hooligan

The plastic hooligan has all the Stone Island gear and considers himself to be a double hard bastard. He is frequently seen hanging around train stations and pubs on match days, usually with a couple of hangers on with the same delusions as him. He has only ever been heard to utter two sentences in public and only ever when he is mob handed 'Get the stragglers' and 'Have you got the time mate?'

He holds all replica shirt wearers in the same contempt with which the proper hooligans hold him, especially the lads he knew at school who could chin him easily. Once his match day experience of keeping well out of the way of any possible harm while simultaneously shouting the loudest is over, he may engage a potential girlfriend in some flirtatious banter. This is then subtly followed up with a dinner invitation; 'half seven at the kebab shop on the high street' once he finishes 'running' the opposition.

The Comedian

This bloke (and believe me it's always a bloke) is very similar to Billy Nee Pals, except he'll normally have a couple of grinning, inane, easily impressed, fuckwits with him. He will spend the match shouting remarks at opposing players and officials that he and his friends think are hysterical. The supporters around him will tend to ignore him as he goes through his routine and tells the poor unfortunates near him how 'I'm mad me.'

Recent examples of this blokes humour include the hysterical 'Ref man get a life ha ha' and the rib popping 'Mario, you're not even super ha ha.'

Try not to split your sides laughing if you are ever seated near a comedian.

The Elitist

This person is male and hates everyone in the ground who 'wasn't there when we were shit', especially the new breed Sky generation. He gets particularly annoyed at people who get in his way by coming into the match after kick off and then leaving ten minutes early. He resents being unable to get a pie and a pint at half time because 'the queue's ower big and full of part timers and success supporters man' and he will tell you the same tales of travelling away to games time and again.

The Elitist has been supporting his team up and down this sceptred isle for the last thirty years - you're reading his story.

Second Half

LOSING MY RELIGION

The Souness Era

The End of the Knight

On 28th August 2004 we lost four - two at Aston Villa, it was the beginning of the end for Sir Bobby. We'd had a bout of conjunctivitis just before the start of the season that had disrupted the build up combined with various injury problems and rumours of players being bought and sold without the manager's knowledge - not the last time that happened either eh?

Following the thirteen and a half million pound sale of Jonathan Woodgate to Real Madrid and the uproar it caused amongst the supporters we started acquiring, what looked on the surface, some decent enough players. Woody's was a sale I applauded incidentally as it was good money for an injury prone player. He was the best centre half I'd seen at the club but just didn't play enough. The reasonably cheap acquisitions of Nicky Butt and Patrick Kluivert from Manchester United and Barcelona respectively were followed by an audacious bid for Everton starlet Wayne Rooney. It's fair to assume that this was who Shepherd had meant when he'd referred to the supporters being 'pleasantly surprised' at who was coming in after Woodgate's departure, although it was blatantly obvious he was never coming.

However, much of this recruitment drive was obviously taking place above Sir Bobby's head as it became increasingly clear that the relationship between manager and board was becoming distant. When Shepherd stupidly announced that this season would be Robson's last at the Newcastle helm the former Ipswich Town, Barcelona and England manager lost almost all control over team affairs. My opinion was, and still is, that if he had thought that Bobby had lost it or needed replacing then he should have had the bollocks to do it there and then rather than his usual compromise after the transfer budget had been spent.

This left Bobby's position untenable and with chaos reigning at the top, those at the bottom began to run amok. Kieron Dyer, that star of the tabloid front pages, was first to endear himself to the Geordie public by refusing to play on the right hand side of midfield and then dropping the Captain's arm-band on the pitch when it was offered to him. An apology fol-lowed but the damage was done, Robson was no longer in command of his troops. Kluivert and Craig Bellamy also wran-gled about who should play where, with the Welsh interna-tional even advising the club not to bother with Rooney, sug-gesting some money be spent on the defence instead - mind you he wasn't fucking wrong was he? In the event we got nei-ther Rooney or a replacement for Woodgate and Robson's fate was sealed by Freddy's short term, cash in the bank, thinking.

The pressure had been building up in the press about his job being in jeopardy and when the teams came out at Villa and Shearer was on the bench you could sense the vultures cir-cling. The fact that he deserved to be on the bench was irrele-vant, you knew how the press would spin it and compare it to when Mad Ruud lost the plot. Worse still, we all knew what the outcome would be. In the end we lost the match but we could-n't have been unluckier. Kluivert went off with a bad injury, their keeper handled outside the box and denied us a clear goal scoring opportunity but only got a yellow card and they scored some flukey deflected goals. Shearer was pictured laughing and joking on the bench and that was that.

Me? I just went to the pub after the match and hoped it would be alright. The press did what they do best and went into negative spin mode. The more gullible, and possibly more recent, supporters fell for it and called for the manager's head and the chairman's knee jerked...hard...as usual.

It was a sad end for an esteemed manager, a man who was black and white through and through and who had dragged us from the lower reaches of the league to regular European qual-ification. He had given us back our pride, many memorable matches in both domestic football and the Champions League and had served us up the football we loved, attacking pacy stuff that helped you forget about the working week.

Devastated as he obviously was, the great man, as ever, behaved with dignity:-

'I am massively disappointed not to be able to finish the job I came here to do,' said Robson, 'I have immensely enjoyed my time here as manager and I wish the club all the best of success in the future. At the present moment I have absolutely nothing to say except to thank the Geordie fans for their tremendous enthusiasm, loyalty and support.'

Anyone expecting Mr. Shepherd to have a successor nailed on and in place would have been disappointed, we didn't do things like that. Various names were bandied around in the press as Shepherd blustered about 'world class names' coming to St. James. In the event it was a little disappointing when the new manager was announced...Graeme Fucking Souness!

This was a man currently managing a team that was below us in the league and who was about to be sacked himself. We were going to give Blackburn compensation for taking him off their hands, they must have been pissing themselves.

Of all the stupid, crass and, frankly unforgiveable, decisions that Shepherd had made over the years this was the most unfathomable and ridiculous. Souness was known throughout football for having no man-management skills, for falling out with star players and for being a 'money' manager. John Carver took control of the team for one game in the intervening period between the official appointment of Souness and the dismissal of Sir Bob - the opposition? Only Blackburn Rovers. I was in Blackpool on a stag do at the time and had a bet on us winning three nil and Shearer getting the first goal. Shearer got the second one and we won three nil, I was a bit gutted until it was pointed out to me that our first was in fact an own goal and Ladbrokes didn't count them. So mortal drunk I went to the bookies to argue my case and came out two hundred quid richer - magic. The bars of Blackpool made a bit more money that night.

Anyway, that aside, the main talking point of the match was that even though Blackburn were shite, their fans were mighty happy to have got rid of their manager and found it highly amusing that we'd taken him on. They predicted that he'd wreck our club and destroy a team that had finished in the top five three years in a row. Sour grapes? Unfortunately not.

On his appointment Souness came out with all the right stuff.

'I'm really pleased my son will grow up with a geordie accent.'

'Best squad of players I've ever managed.'

Etcetera, etcetera.

The man had a falseness about him that belied his perceived status as a straight talking, old school style of player. In fact I am of the opinion that he learnt his press techniques straight from Tony Blair and he certainly displayed more spin than my washing machine. The fallouts weren't long in coming either. In Craig Bellamy, Robson had moulded a match winner. He was a hot headed, rash young man who you may not have wanted to go for a drink with but on the football pitch he was like lightning. He formed one half of a striking partnership with Shearer that compared favourably with the great combos of the past and had scored the goal that took us through to the second stages of the Champions League for the first time in our history.

Graeme Souness played him as a right winger.

We played Crystal Palace away and won two-nil with a couple of decent goals scored by Bellamy and Kluivert in the absence of an injured Shearer. Souness's response was to say that 'the main man (Shearer) will be back next week.' He was and Bellamy was back on the wing - not the greatest example of man management. Bellamy soon became tired of being Souness's whipping boy and reacted as you'd expect a spoilt, cosseted, modern day footballer to react - he threw his toys out of the pram at Arsenal and allegedly refused to play.

Souness had engineered this spat to prove how hard he was and he took his chance, sending our best forward on loan to Celtic and effectively finishing his career at Newcastle and our season in the process. Laurent Robert was next to be told through the local press that he wasn't good enough and we started seeing Shola Ameobi playing on the left wing. All the while the Souness apologists and friends in the press were sticking up for him as he dismantled a team that was the third best in England only a year previously. He talked down Bellamy's value saying he would never play for the club again, ensuring we got nowhere near his true worth when he was eventually sold to Blackburn for peanuts. Then he brought old Liverpool mate Terry McDermott back to the club and his first action was to slag off Bellamy, even though he admitted he'd never met him. The spin and hypocrisy being peddled from the corridors of power at St. James was starting to leave a nasty taste in the mouth as numerous pundits and ex players were wheeled out to talk up Souness's management credentials. The most shameful of these, for me anyway, was Robert Lee. He was on the back pages of some shit rag claiming that 'I would have loved to have played under Souness' and some fans bought the lie and lapped that nonsense up.

And the Chairman and directors of the club? They said this:-

'We had to sack Bobby Robson because he was taking us down'

And yet only a few months earlier they had said this :-

'The directors wish to thank Sir Bobby for the way in

which he has worked tirelessly over the past five years to try to bring success to the club.'

'The club will no doubt continue to benefit from the knowledge and experience he has given during his time here.'

And then the coup-de-grace from Shepherd when asked why he employed Souness rather than the type of manager that would have worked on Tyneside (ie a good one).

'Graeme got the job because he was the one who wanted it the most.'

Fucking brilliant that.

It was nowt to do with the money obviously and it's not even true, I can think of at least fifty two thousand people who wanted it more than him at that point. The football we watched was dire, the results becoming ever more woeful and as predicted, he started spending money like it was going out of fashion. Fifty million pounds left the Newcastle United bank account to acquire the 'talents' of the likes of Boumsong, Luque, Parker, Emre, Faye (Jesus Christ) and Moore. I purposefully left Michael Owen out of that list because he is a class act but a handful of games in three years told it's own story - nice one Graeme.

At the end of his first season I could take no more. I was doing a five hundred mile round trip to watch boring, depressing football. My team was populated by mercenaries, has beens and never will be's. The 'management' of the team was in the hands of a clueless dictator who lurched from crisis to crisis bolstered by his entourage of yes men (Saunders, Murray et al) and spouting soundbite after soundbite to his tame journalists about 'proper players'.

After he came out with most ludicrous statement I have ever heard from anyone anywhere at anytime I knew I had to act.

The statement that finished me?

It was this load of shite and it went shamefully unchallenged by any journalist :-

'I am the most attack minded manager this club has ever had.'

What more attack minded than Kevin 'Lets play a 1-1-9 formation today lads' Keegan or more attack minded than Bobby 'Newcastle 8-0 Sheff Wed' Robson? Fuck off and stop insulting my intelligence you clueless, nepotistic chancer.

It was over for me until he went - I'd loved, supported and defended my club for nigh on thirty years. I'd stood on the terraces in all kinds of shit weather, spent money I didn't have and had seen relationships fall by the wayside.
Now it was finished I wouldn't give Shepherd another pound of my money until Souness was gone..

Wigan (a) 04-05

My self imposed ban on going to home matches was in full effect now and as a result I was suffering withdrawal symptoms from the match day crack. So when my mate gave me a buzz and asked if I fancied a night out in Wigan with the lads I jumped at it. Reasoning that the match would be shite and Souness would play for a draw but I'd still have a night out somewhere I'd never been and I wouldn't be putting any money in Shepherd's pocket no matter how many pies I ate.

We headed up there early doors on the day of the match, miraculously finding the hotel first go, but getting there too early to check in. The hotel itself was a bit grim, facing a graveyard and the housing estate around it didn't look too clever either. Ignoring our precarious surroundings we headed into town to get a bit of breakfast and kill some time until we could throw our gear in our rooms. After we'd passed the third boarded up pub with scorch marks up the brickwork we began to realise why taking the cheapest option isn't always the best and once a local had informed us that our hotel used to be a brothel we decided that there'd be no splitting up that night - no matter how drunk we got.

The town centre was okay and the breakfast we had was cheap and huge, just the way I like them. One thing I noticed though was that every other bloke was massive - maybe they were brought up on Wigan breakfasts? We had another meander back through Beirut to the hotel and got checked in before heading back out for the obligatory pre-match pints.

This was where the banter really started, we gave a bit of cheek to an awfully big bouncer who wouldn't let us in a boozer as we were blatantly far too skinny to be local boys before hitting a big one near the ground that was full of Geordies. The lads started arsing about with their bluetooth phones and discovered that someone in the immediate vicinity had named his phone 'donkey dick'.

Eager to teach the knob a lesson one of the lads sent him some porn via the aforementioned bluetooth. A little beep from behind us followed by a 'Who's Big George and why are you getting that filth?' question from an outraged girlfriend was swiftly followed by a slap round the head and a meek boyfriend trying to placate her with 'Honest I haven't a clue who's sending me that.' It's hard to keep a straight face when you're watching a seven stone student getting a hiding off his bird in front of his mates.

Donkey Dick? Just Dick would suffice I think.

The match itself was shite and we got beat, that was the Souness way though and I expected nothing less, the main entertainment was in winding up the Wigan fans. The majority of them weren't really used to big sets of away fans and seemed more interested in us than the game, some of them were kindly pointing to their throats and making slashing gestures, presumably to tell us not to eat too many Wigan breakfasts so we didn't get as fat as them. A few of their younger element, dressed in Burberry, took pictures of us on their camera phones and then made similar gestures. I can only assume that was to show their girlfriends when they got home so as to get them in the mood for love or something.

Anyway, the main laugh of the match was when an obviously steroid riddled Wigan gentlemen decided to show us that they weren't all pie eating, rugby playing fat bastards and took his top off to invite us to some kind of 'who can take the most body building drugs' competition. Needless to say after five or six thousand of us laughed at him and mentioned his tits he quickly hoyed it back on again.

There's always one isn't there?

I'm just glad it's not me any more.

After the match we got back into town for a few pints and had some quality banter with some locals then headed back to the hotel. A few vodkas later and we were back in town and seriously on the lash, most of it's a blur bar one bizarre little incident. The big bouncer from earlier turned up when we were in a bar and decided to enlist us in his campaign against every other bouncer in town. He swept as many of us up in his arms as he could and ran towards the doormen shouting 'come on Geordies let's get them' - unfortunately for him I think they were expecting this, as we sidestepped his lunge, and they pushed him into the road. The last I saw of him I think he was on the receiving end of some 'reasonable force'.

And that was it, no points, no money left, a longish journey the next day with a hangover and people screaming for the car to pull over so they could be sick.

And do you know what?

I wouldn't have missed it for the world.

Better late than never

I pulled into my street at about half six on Christmas Morning, the journey seemed to have taken seconds but in the preceding four hours I'd looked back over thirty years of memories and enjoyed every minute of it. In my mind's eye I'd travelled the length and breadth of our fine country and remembered stories from every corner of it - granted they normally involved strong drink and me making an arse of myself but hey, they were still entertaining eh?

I'd seen nothing but darkness on the motorway all the way back, I hadn't even caught sight of Santa - mind you that was just as well, you don't get your presents if you see him do you? But, as I killed the engine and got out of the car, I looked up and saw the biggest star I can remember, honestly I nearly burst into a hymn it was that big and bright, and Col's words echoed round my head once more.

'We should write a book Rivs...'

I got into the house, quickly necked Santa's sherry and headed upstairs to give our lass a kiss.

'People like me don't write books' I thought.

Scrotes from Byker that used to run round with no knees in their trousers or food in their bellies tend to work in warehouses and factories not mix with the glitterati at the Bookers (maybe a touch optimistic for a book about the toon but you get the idea). Then I thought back to the bloke I'd just buried less than eighteen hours ago - he would have done it if he'd had the chance so why shouldn't I? I'd just entertained myself for four hours on a dark motorway with memories of matches gone by so why couldn't I just jot them down and see what happened?

I'd even missed out stuff like the nine hour coach journey to Bournemouth where we'd been swigging Vodka from a coke bottle and fallen asleep, getting into the ground fifteen minutes after kick off and missing our goal (Quinny - who else) before losing two-one and having the journey back with a hangover. Or when we'd gone to Hull and been attacked in a boozer but I'd been so mortal I hadn't even noticed. What about the time we'd ended up in Morecambe after the Tranmere game and scared the life out of that bullying bouncer, that was brilliant, or the time I'd got lost in Sheffield after the Wednesday match and had to be rescued from an angry mob or the time when...well, you get the picture.

I resolved there and then, no matter how long it took, I'd write this book. But first things first, as my head hit the pillow I decided that as soon as Christmas was out of the way I was going to write to the Newcastle fanzines and let them know that one of their own had gone to the great Cup Final in the sky. Col's passing was sad and untimely but, perversely, gave me the courage to have a go at something I'd always secretly dreamed of doing and has fortified me against rejection along the way. I've added to this book from that point and tried to cover the post Col years. It's not the same at the match now without him but then I don't think it's the same at any game now for the lads of my era, the great God of television has seen to that.

My first attempt at writing anything was rubbish, basically because I didn't know what I wanted to say or how to say it so, realising that I needed guidance, I did what everyone in this day and age does...I consulted Google. I typed 'writing' into the search engine and discovered a site run by the BBC called 'Get Writing' there were people there who advised, encouraged and helped you and I was away. I posted loads of stuff and got instant feedback, helping me to learn rapidly. Obviously looking back now I think most of it was shite but I was on a steep learning curve and enjoying myself - that was enough for me at the time.

Following that came my proudest moment, the article I wrote about Col and me was accepted by 'The Mag' and became my first ever published work - I've still got the copy they sent me and I show it to everyone who's interested (and a lot who aren't). I got a little more confident then and started writing my first book, actually based on some of the stuff you've read in here, and learned quickly about the harsh world of publishing. Agents rejected me left, right and centre as my stuff didn't fit into the rigid literary pigeonholes required by the big publishers or bookshops. One agent rang me personally to tell me how much he loved my book, how the dialogue was brilliant and my eye for 'local colour' was outstanding but he didn't think he could sell it so he wasn't going to bother - I didn't know whether to laugh or cry.

A little later in the year, whilst slagging off Souness on a Newcastle message board I accepted an invitation to become a regular columnist in a new North East Football magazine (Players Inc) and embraced the opportunity with relish, little realising it would spark off the recollections of matches, days out and misdemeanours that would fill this book. As Souness managed to somehow make going to the match boring I found a new outlet for the passion and the pride - I started writing about it, hoping that one day anyone who was interested (or daft enough) would want to read the book that followed.

Boro and Palace (h) - 04/05

These two matches happened in the same week and are, for me, synonomous with the whole of the Souness era at Newcastle. They were both at home, both very winnable and in both games he played one man up front in an attempt to stifle the opposition - wanker. Nothing of note happened on the football side in either game, apart from the predictable nil-nil that tends to occur when you don't set out to score goals, but in the second of them - at home to Palace - something fairly unprecedented occurred off the pitch...the crowd stopped watching the game.

In a flawed advertising campaign some bright spark decided to stick adverts to the back of every seat but at half time a very bored crowd took to making paper aeroplanes and trying to throw them into the goals in an effort to amuse themselves. This continued after the teams came back out and the game had restarted. The high point of the entire match and the occasion that got the biggest cheer was when a particularly good effort from high up in the Leazes/Sir John Hall stand ended up in the net. Mine didn't even make the pitch - mind you I swiped one off a little kid that made the front row.

Some time after that a local radio station invited people to send their questions to the 'manager' (he'll never be a manager as long as I've got a hole in my arse!) and I sent the following:-

I would like to know how you qualify the ludicrous statement you came out with a while back about being 'the most attack minded manager this club has had'. I ask this after watching two nil nil draws, both at home where we played with one man up front. In the second of these games (Palace) the fans resorted to making paper aeroplanes for amusement, I don't recall ever doing that under Keegan or Robson - so please explain your statement to me.

Andy Rivers

I never got an answer to this as the interview was 'postponed for unforeseen circumstances'. However, a local newspaper (you know which one) that had very close links with the then hierarchy at St. James ran a big spread proclaiming that they would put our questions to Souness.

So, whilst not believing it would actually happen, I had another go and posted the same question. Inexplicably it appeared in the paper but had been edited down to the following:-

I would like to know how you qualify the ludicrous statement you came out with a while back about being the most attacked-minded manager this club has had. I ask this after watching two goalless draws, both at home, when we played with one man up front. - Andy Rivers

This allowed Souness to avoid the embarrassment of explaining why the fans were so bored they had to learn origami to amuse themselves and also saved him from telling us why he was a much better manager than either Keegan or Robson. Incidentally I'm of the opinion that it also meant the paper in question didn't upset the hierarchy at St. James too much and thus didn't jeopardise their cosy little 'club insider' stories - that's just my opinion mind.

Anyway, here is what the David Brent of football management answered to the half of my question that actually got printed:-

The way we play depends on how you choose to see it. We played with three strikers against Middlesbrough and Crystal Palace but we didn't win either game because we did not convert our chances. It's nothing to do with systems. But what it has to do with is individuals on the night not taking their chances.

Graeme Souness

Now some of you might not remember these games but I do and when he says we played with three strikers on the night he is, strictly speaking, correct.

However, when I point out that of these three 'strikers' only one of them, the by now highly immobile Alan Shearer, played in any kind of forward position, Ameobi played in left midfield and was replaced in that position by striker number three (Kluivert), you may get an idea of the kind of spin this man and his media buddies employed at every opportunity.

A Man of Letters

I'd had enough by now and felt it was time to let the Club Chairman know how I felt and what I was going to do about it. Here's a copy of a letter I sent to Freddy Shepherd. I'm guessing it was filed in the bin by some club flunkey without him ever seeing it - a bit like Robert Mugabe and election results - but I felt better for doing it and I was sure Col would have approved.

20 April 2005

Reference: Season Ticket Renewal

Mr. F. Shepherd

Newcastle United Football Club

St. James Park

Newcastle upon Tyne

NE1 4ST

Dear Mr. Shepherd,

With regard to my application for season ticket renewal 2005-2006. Unfortunately I will be unable to bring myself to renew my ticket, or indeed spend any money at all on club merchandise, whilst the present manager and his team are on the payroll. I am thirty-four years old and began supporting the club in 1976 at the age of six. I have been there through good times and bad; I was in the Gallowgate End when we were relegated in eighty nine and also there for the farcical playoff game against Sunderland in nineteen ninety.

I have seen us throw away three nil half time leads and snatch defeat from the jaws of victory many times. In short I have known despair and heartache at this club.

I have to say though that until last week I have never felt the anger and frustration at the ineptitude of one of our managers and my own team in such waves. The sheer lack of spine and will to win displayed by the players allied with the couldn't care less attitude that has been on show all season was galling in the extreme. This has I believe been exacerbated by the incompetent management of team affairs by the manager and his cronies on the backroom staff. We have so many coaches now and yet players are going backwards in technique and basic skills. As a team we cannot pass or keep the ball. Our tactics are to use our goalkeeper as a playmaker and lump it up to our centre forward and hope for the best. Defending is an alien concept and panic sets in whenever the ball is in our half (often).

I have heard all of the excuses and sound bites from the manager all season and am now heartily sick of them. He has changed from it being the best squad he's ever worked with to needing a whole new team. Everything is Laurent Robert, Craig Bellamy or Bobby Robsons fault, has the man no idea of taking the consequences for your own actions?

I am also very, very tired of listening to his ex-Liverpool apologists and golf buddies in the media finding new reasons why we under perform, the club is now more governed by spin than any political party.

This season has been an absolute disgrace resulting in my club being the laughing stock of football once again. From sacking the manager a couple of weeks into the season after he had spent the transfer budget for the summer to appointing the most derided manager in the premiership from a club below us in the league. From the smokescreen transfer bid for Wayne Rooney, a player we would never have got, to the contrived dismissal of Craig Bellamy, a player who at least tried and had a backbone but wasn't one of the managers favourites. From the giving of a new contract to O Brien when he isn't worth a place in the team and hasn't been all season to the slating of all the youth players only this morning in the papers.

It is apparent that if you are 'in' with the manager and his staff then you can do no wrong - Dyer, Bowyer, O'Brien etc. If however, he or his staff don't like you then you are out no matter how important to the team. Bellamy, Robert (UEFA Cup quarter final) and as we found out this morning anyone under twenty one. I have now decided I have had enough, it will be hard for me but I cannot justify spending fortunes on a team that neither appreciate it nor care. I realise that my frustration and exasperation will not bother you in the slightest but you need to realise that I am not from the 'Sky' generation and am in fact indicative of the legion of thirty and forty something blokes who have grown up with Newcastle United. We are the backbone of this club and have been taken for granted too many times now, you should think seriously about that before dismissing this letter.

To sum up I would like to point out that while the bumbling, inept, confrontational, excuse for a premiership manager continues in his position, along with what seems a bigger entourage than Mariah Carey then I shall not be attending home matches.

Newcastle is, has been and always will be my club. It represents my city and my people but is little more than a national laughing stock at present. I suggest you check out a few of the independent websites and message boards to gauge the feeling among supporters. There is a swell of dislike and discontent building up towards the club and management, yourself included, the like of which I have never seen before. I urge you to act before it's too late and appoint a proper manager to do a proper job.

Thank you for your time

Yours sincerely

Andy Rivers

And here's another one I was forced to send a few months later. They'd obviously read my previous letter carefully, laughed at it and sent my renewal application out without a second thought. I'm only surprised they didn't write MUG across it in big capital letters.

2nd June 2005

Reference: Season Ticket Renewal

The Box Office

Newcastle United Football Club

St. James Park

Newcastle upon Tyne

NE1 4ST

To whom it may concern

Many thanks for your letter inviting me to renew my season ticket, unfortunately I shall be unable to either renew or attend St. James for the foreseeable future. I did write to the chairman and tell him why about a month ago (letter attached) but my letter was probably filed in the bin.

As nothing has changed apart from the ludicrous sale of one our more solid, professional and versatile defenders for £1m and the promise (never heard this one before) that I will be 'astounded' by our new signings, undoubtedly from Blackburn Rovers or Glasgow Rangers, then I see no reason to change my mind.

Yours sincerely

Andy Rivers

West Ham (h) 05-06

My vow to chuck it all in and only go to away games from here on in lasted about three months...I was there for the first home game of the next season. In doing so I admit that made me part of the problem at Newcastle under the Shepherd era; as long as the fans kept turning up then he wasn't that bothered and we did, and still do, keep turning up.

When I went though I did it knowing we'd be shit. The team was criminally light in the forward positions with only an ageing Shearer, an over rated Ameobi and a couple of young reserves as recognisable strikers. Despite having the whole of the previous season and three months of the summer to plan their purchases the manager and chairman felt that they should wait until the very last moment of the transfer window before spunking all of our budget on panic buys.

Thus we went into this game with nothing likely to cause West Ham any bother at their end, in other words a typical Souness game. We drew nil-nil in an absolutely dire match. The best players on show were both with the visitors, Reo-Coker and the virtual pensioner Sheringham, and the crowd were not happy at the end. Me? I was just bored. Souness had sucked the life out of my club. It was becoming a chore for me now and I was going more for the day out on the drink than for the actual football.

As the end of the transfer window loomed large and results continued to disappoint, the dynamic duo acted. Firstly they lashed out the thick end of ten million quid on Albert Luque, the highly rated Spanish international, and then paid seventeen million pounds for Michael Owen, before bringing Nobby Solano home from Aston Villa. On paper these looked good, if not expensive, signings but reading between the lines it was obvious that things weren't all hunky dory. Luque has since admitted that he had barely heard of Newcastle and only came for the money - believe me if you'd watched him play for us you'd have known that anyway. Owen wanted to go back to Liverpool, they wouldn't pay over seven million pounds for him and so Freddy used a sledgehammer to crack a nut, claiming he had some sort of special relationship with Real Madrid that enabled us to bring Owen to Tyneside. Errm no Freddie - I think you'll find it was the extra ten million pounds that swung the deal and given Owen's appearance record for us since his move you can see Liverpool's point.

The signing of Owen was a particular low point for me as Shepherd and Souness celebrated having more money than Liverpool with a cringeworthy spectacle of self indulgence when he actually put pen to paper. Sky Sports News were present to record the momentous occasion of Newcastle acquiring a player and a couple of thousand kids, who were off school that week, obliged the cameras with some scripted chanting. Shepherd and Souness milked the moment and Owen, looking suitably embarrassed, trailed behind them. One commentator summed up the whole debacle, in fact the whole ethos of the Shepherd reign, succinctly.

'Other clubs celebrate trophies, Newcastle United celebrate trophy signings.'

That was us under Shepherd in a nutshell and it was fucking embarrassing.

Man City (a) 05/06

Things couldn't go on as they were. Souness had lost the fans
(not that he'd ever really had us in the first place), the players
and, with the advent of this match, finally, the boardroom. It
was a typical Newcastle performance under the 'management'
of Souness, typical in that we lost, we never looked like scoring a goal and the players just gave up.

He responded by saying he wouldn't quit which, as we all
know, is manager speak for I'm hanging on for the cheque.

Freddy Shepherd was quoted after this game as saying the
moment he'd known it was time to get rid of Souness was
when three of our players collided in the centre circle. He obviously hadn't noticed the big 'Souness Out' banner hung from
the visting fans end at Eastlands. He'd obviously had his radio
turned up really loud in his car when the Newcastle fans were
banging on his roof demanding the Scottish one's removal
after the shameful capitulation in the league cup against
Wigan reserves. He obviously hadn't noticed the fifty million
quid wasted on players during the sixteen months of Souness's
tenure and he'd obviously not watched any games during that
time if this was the only match in which he thought the self
acclaimed hard man of British football might not be up to the
job.

Following Souness's sacking his assistant Dean 'do you
want a cup of tea gaffer' Saunders was suspended on full salary
ahead of his own big pay off. They both didn't do too badly
considering they'd only managed to win a grand total of thirty
six games in eighty three attempts and this mark you in a season when we'd been in the UEFA cup and playing the likes of
FC Gardenshed and The Horse and Jockey B Team.

For me personally it felt like a weight had been lifted from
my shoulders. The black cloud that had enveloped me every
time I thought about the toon was instantly dissipated and I
felt positive about anything and everything. The almost daily
rejection letters I was getting from agents for 'Maxwell's Silver

Hammer', my first attempt at a novel, were like water off a duck's back now he was gone.

I tore into my next book with relish. 'Special' took shape amid a backdrop of committed performances from the lads, we were a team again and it helped me enormously. All the while I'd been writing these novels I'd been half thinking that I was fooling myself, that a radgy like me shouldn't be trying to do this but in a way Souness convinced me that I should.

During his spell at the Toon I'd read some crap books (football as well as fiction) as well as some excellent writing in various fanzines that gripped me much more than ridiculous falsified hooligan accounts. This made me realise that, as I was quite capable of writing well enough to appear in these publications then I could also match, and even better, some of these books. So in the same way that Souness is considered a football manager alongside true greats like Sir Bobby Robson and Sir Alex Ferguson then I could certainly be considered a writer alongside the likes of Irvine Welsh and Christopher Brookmyre. Suitably inspired I got on with it - I might never get anywhere but it couldn't hurt to have a go could it? I might be the literary equivalent of 'George Weahs Cousin' and be found out quickly but I'd still have made my mark.

At the time of writing neither Souness nor his favourite yes man (do you want biscuits with the tea gaffer? Shall I make an offer to Rangers of nine million for their biscuits - you'll get the money back in shares then?) have been employed anywhere meaningful and it appears now that even club chairmen have wised up to just how shite, out of touch and generally incompetent they really are.

Souness has since been heard on Irish radio with the equally loathsome Eamonn Dunphy slagging off Newcastle Fans and Keegan respectively which just shows the mark of the man.

Spoiled, arrogant and deluded. Newcastle United is well rid of this charlatan.

COME BACK AROUND

Villa (a) 05-06

In common with lots of you I served my apprenticeship at my team pre-Premiership. I started going to the match with my mates in the early eighties and we used to spend all week at school excitedly discussing who we'd be playing, which star names would be torturing us that weekend and how we could get some drink before the match.

My abiding memory of those days, and indeed pretty much up to the present time, were of the lads attacking in waves and being shite at the back. From Arthur Cox's three musketeers up front, through Willie McFaul's Goddard and Beardsley combination, taking in the mighty Quinn and the much under-rated David Kelly and Gavin Peacock and all the way through the Keegan years we have usually had a go. As a team we've never won owt in all that time and have consistently shot ourselves in the foot BUT we always had a go and as fans we were entertained and heartened by the efforts being made in our name.

Yes, there have been aberrations on the way, the Dalglish era was one of grim and uninspiring football but it did result in our first Cup Final for twenty four years. The Gullit period also got us to a Cup Final and we scored the odd goal now and then, so maybe it wasn't that bad eh? The Robson years? In the main they were magic, he took a dispirited, relegation threatened team and made us the third best team in England, got us into the Champions League second stage and along the way we gave out some right hidings (Sheff Wed, Spurs in the cup etc.)

So all in all, looking back over my Newcastle history, I can say we generally had a go and have never lain down and died, whoever the opposition (except at Wembley obviously) and despite the fact we've never won anything I've always had a good time.

From standing in the scoreboard end hoping we might snatch something against Liverpool (good old George Reilly) to being rat arsed in Peterborough as Keegan's cavaliers swept all before them. No matter how bad my week, how boring my job was I always had the match to look forward to. Got a final written warning on Monday? Doesn't matter, I've got a ticket for Villa on Saturday. Bright red reminder for the phone bill? Don't care, cos we're seventh in the league and we'll hammer Barnsley. You get the picture right?

Well under Souness it was never like that, in fact if anything it was the other way round. The last sixteen months under the boring one had been a catalogue of poor performances, excuses, boring football, excuses, un-needed confrontations, excuses, expensive flops, excuses, spineless capitulation and above all excuses. I was nearing the end of my tether before his dismissal, not anger or rage at his incompetence but apathy, I was just going through the motions at the match and I wasn't the only one. Everyone was going to the game expecting us to get beat, play poorly and then read afterwards that it was all someone else's fault and that Souness was happy with his 'proper players'.

For the first time in thirty years I wasn't that bothered if I went to the match or not. Where once I'd have had to have been unconscious, with both my legs cut off and in the middle of the Atlantic to have even contemplated missing the kick off. In the final days of Souness's reign I was having 'just one more' in the pre match boozer just to cut short the time I had to spend being depressed by the spineless shambles that my team had become.

But, as the saying goes, it's always darkest before the dawn and as we all know Freddy eventually had to hold his hands up and admit he'd made a mistake. Appointing Wor Glen and Big Al as the caretaker team was, at the time and given the lowly position we were in, a bit of very good fortune on his part. Two Newcastle captains both ex and current meant that they, above everyone else, knew exactly how much it mattered and the change in the team was immediate and apparent.

From the first minute of their first game in charge the lads were up for it. Tackles flying in, seventy / thirty challenges being made and won and goals being scored. Despite Souness's protestations and all of the articles by players about being behind him I believed, and still do, the evidence of my own eyes. From the minute he, having secured his unearned wedge, was dragged kicking and screaming out of St. James Park there was a huge upsurge in determination from the team. Something I never saw when he was in charge and this can only lead me to think that not everyone was behind the manager in the so called 'happy' dressing room.

The proof that Glenn and Alan had changed things and that we were heading in the right direction again was the Aston Villa away game in this season. Our lass was away for the weekend and I had a seventy two hour pass - I was hopeful of a decent performance, if not a result, but even a good hiding off Villa wouldn't spoil it as long as we had a go. The talk in the boozer beforehand was of whether we could get a draw, I, ever the optimist declared I'd be having a whole fiver on us winning. When pressed I even stated the score line and first scorer. I'd be going two one to us and Shola for first goal.

My reasoning was simple. I was drunk.

Imagine my surprise as we entered the ground late (transport to and from Villa Park on a match day is bloody hard work - England's second city my arse) and took our seats (well stood next to them) only to see the Gosforth Lion slide rule a pass to the Fenham Eusebio for him to score the opening goal.

Everyone jumped on me, stupidly thinking we might win - nutters. Normal service was resumed when Luke Moore pulled one back for them following our trademark shocking marking at a set piece and I just hoped we could weather the storm. The odd lunatic pointed out that my bet was still on and asked what price I'd got, I told them the eighty to one odds but obviously stated quite categorically that I'd be happy with a draw at this stage as we needed the points. Then on the half hour N'Zogbia scored and we were two one up - GET IN! BOLLOCKS TO THE DRAW MAN ME BET'S ON!!!!

There was an hour of the match to go and I was screaming for the whistle - everyone around me was more interested in my bet than the game and I was starting to lose my voice. Another sixty minutes of hell beckoned. We were tidy enough in the second half, in fact my only concern was that we might go mental and get a third, but that all changed in the sixty first minute when Babayaro, showing an appetite for the battle for once, got himself sent off and, even worse, conceded a penalty. I had the betting slip in my hand and was ready to launch it but something told me not to (in-built tightness I reckon) and seconds later Given only saved it to a mighty roar from the travelling support - well everyone but me as my voice had completely gone by this point. Even though there was half an hour left I knew then that we'd won and it allowed me to reflect on the transformation we had undergone since the departure of the divisive Scottish one.

Two-one up, down to ten men and facing a penalty. Under Souness and his 'coaching team/bookies runners' we would have lost this game five or six goals to two (assuming we'd have got two under him in the first place like). Under the Shearer/Roeder combination we rolled our sleeves up, got on with it and fought for every ball like proper men, the team and the supporters were as one and after a long separation we were again Newcastle United. As it turned out that feeling wasn't to last but that's for the next chapter.

More to the point though I was four hundred quid up and had another two days to blow it before our lass came home - good old Shola, always rated him.

Had Enough, Had Enough

By now I had a regular column in Players Inc. Magazine as well as a couple of stories in publications here and there and I was starting to flex my writers muscles (they're not very big - think peas on a bit of string). My optimism and genuine excitement at this new world I'd discovered was tempered by the fact that I was beginning to see the signs of decline in the team again that had been prevalent during the mis-management of the Souness years. It was obvious that Glenn Roeder had been short changed as manager of the toon and was being hung out to dry by the chairman so felt I had to write about it.

An open letter to Freddy Shepherd - Sept 2006

Dear Freddy,

Distinctly underwhelmed, not a phrase I've ever used before in relation to the toon but it perfectly sums up just how I feel about our performance in this summers transfer window. We all knew what was needed, we all assumed by the spin being peddled from the corridors of power at St. James that you knew what was needed and, by midnight on the thirty first of August we all knew that you'd blown it again.

Even through your legendary thick skin you appear to have finally felt the public mood on Tyneside and realised we are not happy with you, hence the huffy statement about having spent fifteen million quid and having nothing to reproach yourself for. Call me pedantic but as we amassed somewhere in the region of seven million pounds through sales (Boumsong £4m, Faye £2m, Chopra and Bowyer £500k each) then we only actually spent around eight million big ones on improving a squad that was threadbare on both quality and numbers even before we lost six players from it. You also stated that it wasn't your fault and it was the transfer window to blame.

Has the window just been in operation this year then?

Is it only us who has to abide by it and everyone else can just do what they want, leaving us at a disadvantage?

No Freddy it's not, you knew the rules the same as everyone else and you knew you had three months to get in the players targeted by your manager. That you failed to do so is not the fault of anyone else. You are the extremely well paid head honcho at the club that is being turned down by players of the ilk of Robert Huth (lumbering carthorse who turns slower than a supertanker in the pacific) and the buck stops with you.

Let's have a look at the personnel you actually managed to bring in shall we: -

Damien Duff - class act, great price but why? We already had Charlie N'zogbia, who in many people's eyes was our player of the season last year, and the emerging Alan O Brien, Duffs most likely successor in the Republic of Ireland squad. Two good young players to cover the left wing/midfield slot in place already; we could have saved five million and then not dicked James Milner around. Incidentally, James Milner, scored the winner for England U21's on a Wednesday and was then left out of our squad totally on the Saturday against Fulham, not worried about any chants of support for the lad were you?

Obafemi Martins - possibly a little over priced and very nervous looking, however, it's obvious he's desperate to do well so I won't argue with this other than to point out the following fact. Your manager specifically said he wanted young and hungry British players with Premiership experience (Andy Johnson anyone?) so who signed the Nigerian who's only ever played in Italy then, you or him?

Guiseppe Rossi - or as he's already known in the stands, Guiseppe Chopra. Ten years ago (just before you became chairman incidentally) we fought off competition from Man Utd for the services of the then best centre forward in the world. Now we've sunk so low as to beg them for their fourth choice striker...for four months? It doesn't matter how good he is really as he's going back to them once we've blooded him.

Olly Bernard - not good enough for Southampton or Rangers (Jesus, even Boumsong was good enough for Rangers) and has left us twice in rows over money, lots to prove.

Antoine Sibierski - I was already depressed by the fact that we were begging players off Man United but at least they've got a very good team and therefore their reserves would rightly struggle to get a game, but a Man City cast off! A thirty two year old Manchester F***king City reserve player, this is the team we finished above in the league during one of our worst seasons in the last twenty years, and he couldn't get a game for them. Appears to have been signed purely because he's six foot two, I wonder what Rob McDonald's doing these days?

Prior to this transfer window I was confident that Glenn Roeder could get us a trophy as long as he was backed in the transfer market. This has patently not been the case, however the recent performances against West Ham, Liverpool and Everton showed enough quality to suggest that he can organise his meagre resources effectively and I'm optimistic that we may just surprise a few people in one of the cups. Mind you, imagine what he could have done if we'd managed to sign a couple of quality defenders and another decent forward, there's only Man Utd playing with any sort of consistency, we could have been up there Pompey style and rattling some of the big four's cages.

In conclusion Freddy I would just like to point out that attendances are starting to drop and tickets are still available the day before the match. You are slowly but surely losing the Geordie public and this should worry you greatly, you might like to bear it in mind come the January transfer window.

Howay the lads

Andy Rivers

Fulham (a) 06/07

The Souness reign was over and Glenn had steadied the ship. Unfortunately, after doing so he was given the job full time but without the assistance of Alan Shearer as the Gosforth lion headed for the comfy chairs of the BBC. The chairman could obviously see his dividends rising if he took the cheap option and despite declaring that 'there's a queue of world class managers for this job' it was Roeder, ex academy head, that got the job. Nice one Freddie. Although strictly speaking we couldn't really hold it against him as none of us actually believed him when he came out with the world class thing, after all we were still waiting to be 'pleasantly surprised' after the sale of Woodgate to Real Madrid.

The season was petering out, the football was average to say the least and the injuries, which Glenn never mentioned - ever, were piling up as certain players started finding reasons not to be on the pitch.

This wasn't the lowest point of my relationship with Newcastle United by any means, that had come a few years earlier when the Scottish clown was employed, but the joy at his removal was long since gone and I was half back to going to the match purely to have a day on the drink with the lads and expected nothing in terms of entertainment or lifted morale. This match didn't change anything - it was shite and we lost, it's only in the book because of what happened beforehand. I even left before the end to get the tube to Islington to meet a load of mates and get on the hoy and in doing so missed our goal (Martins). I still didn't care and wasn't even that bothered if we went down (heresy I know - you're probably lighting the fire as we speak), reasoning that a spell in the lower divisions would rid us of both the chairman and his cash greedy hangers on as well as a lot of the Keegan era bandwagon jumpers. The club I'd fallen in love with thirty years previously was taking me for granted and we were heading for a break up.

It was only a matter of time before I started cheating, you know how it is, you start watching the local non league team 'for a laugh', have a couple of pints and talk some nonsense in the club house and before you know it you're making excuses to be there every Saturday and your lass is getting suspicious - we've all been there lads eh? I wasn't the only one either, the season ticket waiting list at Newcastle was gone - from fifteen thousand to zero in ten years. You could buy tickets the day before the match and home gates were starting to dip under fifty thousand in the league. It looked like the divorce solicitors were going to be making a fortune and the marriage guidance mob were stowed off. If you're reading this Freddie then well done, turning the Geordie public off Newcastle United is really an impossible task to achieve but somehow you were managing it.

Anyway, as I was saying, the real entertainment before this match happened after I'd left the boozer and was making my way to the ground. I'd had six or seven pints and had been out late the previous night, in fact I was still drinking at three in the morning - incidentally I'd also had a cat thrown at me from a distance of about a foot resulting in a scar down my chin that is still visible to this day but that's drinking in a countryside village for you.

However, I digress, I'm making my way to the ground with my brother (yes the Man Utd fan who still goes to toon matches with me just to support the other team - you'd have thought he'd have grown out of this by now wouldn't you) and I'm approached by a camera crew.

Posh bloke with mike: 'Excuse me sir, we're gauging peoples opinions for the Richard and Judy programme'

Me: 'It's shite. Owt else?'

Posh Bloke, smiling as he's heard this all day: 'No, it's to publicise the new book by Stuart Maconie - Pies and Prejudice. We'd like your opinions on the North-South divide.'

Me (brain slowly clicking into gear through the lager fog): 'I write books - would Richard and Judy like to have a look?'

Posh Bloke, smile freezing on face as he hasn't heard this one today and thinks he's about to be bored to death by a fifteen stone, shaven headed, drunken Geordie who thinks he can write: 'Ehhm maybe in the future - do you have any opinions on the North-South divide?'

Me realising I'm going to be on national television and vaguely aware that my brother is tugging on my arm to stop me making an arse of myself: 'Fucking right I do pal.'

What followed was a rant that would have impressed old Adolf himself - I castigated our southern cousins for anything and everything under the sun. You probably missed my impressive performance though as most of it was cut from the show - probably due to the impressive number of expletives I managed to inject into every sentence. The ten or so seconds that remained of my ground breaking television debut is reproduced here, be warned though it's powerful stuff and you should read on with caution:-

Ready for it?

Okay, well don't say I didn't warn you.

'Hoo man, I'll tell you why the North's better than the south...Cos we've got the sexiest accents in the whole world...so you can stick ya cockney right where the sun doesn't shine!!'

I topped off this powerful oratory by making a gun motion with the top two fingers of my right hand, winking and making a clicking noise with my tongue before swaggering off towards the turnstiles - it was magnificent.

The match? As I said - it was crap, we got beat two-one and the beer was as over-priced as ever.

And our lass still isn't speaking to me.

Big Sham 07-08

As you know at the start of season '06 - '07 I sent an open letter to Freddy Shepherd through my column in Players Inc - I'm guessing he didn't read it as the only signing we made in the January transfer window was the loan of American defender Oguchi Onweyu - a six foot four muscle bound pile of shite. Performances weren't good and some investment in the team may have helped, it wasn't to be and we ended that season badly. The manager was disposed of (good luck Glenn - you'll always be one of us) and the team was in the lower reaches of the division.

Shepherd, for once, appeared to have got the timing of his next appointment right - he even seemed to have thought about it (not a given with him). It was to be his last major act as Newcastle United chairman - thank god. The manager he appointed was Sam Allardyce or big Sam to his media mates, an old school player who was, surprisingly, right up to date in his coaching methods. He may not have been everyone's choice but it's fair to say he was probably the best we could have got at the time, we were no longer a European team and rumours of interference with player purchases may well have put a lot of the better managers off working with Shepherd.

Then after the mildly pleasant shock of getting in a proper manager we had the best news I've heard in some years, the previously unknown Mike Ashley was buying up shares in the club and it was obvious that Shepherd and his acolytes couldn't do anything about it. When it became apparent that the cancer was being removed from the heart of the club we love my glee was uncontainable, I may even have got a round in at one point I was so happy. Ashley took over and appointed Chris Mort as his chairman, we became professional again - it was brilliant. There was free pints for fans in the ground, season ticket incentives that included free cup games and interest free credit on the aforementioned tickets. The icing on the cake though, for me anyway, was the news that certain previous board members were no longer welcome at St. James.

Incidentally, when it was reported that after ten long years of enduring the most embarrassing chairman in the premiership (and that takes some doing) Freddy 'you're all mugs for buying the shirts' Shepherd was being removed from his post it was lucky I was in the house. Mainly because I'd have probably been sectioned for running around the aisles at Tescos shouting 'GET IN' and shaking my fist in triumph. Mind you as it was our lass was surprised by my triple back flip - women eh.

Big Sam's first game in charge was at home to Aston Villa (it's always them isn't it) and I'd travelled up from Oxfordshire with my nephew in order to keep the toon fire burning strong in him and to ensure he'd be as miserable as me for the next fifty years - it's character building anyway man.

I'd also started writing this book about my Newcastle exploits by now, as well as a couple more columns on our misadventures in football, so some more material was always going to come in handy. As I'd let my season ticket lapse during the Souness years I was forced to buy some general match day tickets and ended up at the front of the Leazes End(sorry Sir John but it was my club before it was yours and I don't want to change the name - it'll always be the Leazes) right behind the goal. It was a traditional Geordie weekend, basically it was lashing down, windy and cold, and as we were at the front, the roof of the stand was offering us as much protection as the rhythm method offers teenage lovers.

The Villa players were kicking in having finished their warm up and not one of them was anywhere near the target. How we laughed as the balls came flying at us from all angles and I jovially pointed out the inadequacies of the visitors to them every time they came near us. One of their number, some knob called Gardner, who was probably the worst offender had a few more goes at knocking my head off but was so shite he missed every time before having one last effort.

He gave it a mighty clout and it sped toward me like a nuclear rocket on steroids ...before firing straight past and breaking a seat a few rows back, I noticed as the stewards got on the radio that the seat had a plaque attached to it with someone's name on. Some bloke was going to turn up for the first match of the season to find the wet seat he'd paid the thick end of six hundred quid for was bust already - he'd probably think he'd gone to the stadium of shite by mistake.

As the teams came out I confidently pronounced to my nephew that as Villa were so rubbish in front of goal and we'd battered Bolton away in our first game that we'd probably win three or four nowt. Ninety minutes of tedium later and we all knew what to expect over the forthcoming season.

And, most importantly, my nephew now knew what to expect for the rest of his life.

Fast forward a few months into the Allardyce reign and, on the surface at least, things were looking rosy. We seemed solid enough at the back, combative in midfield and the lads at the front were starting to click...this couldn't be our year could it? Nah, course not...I find a reason to think it's our season every time, Jesus you'd think I'd remember that I'm a Magpie not a cockney red. But, whilst I'm eternally optimistic where the toon are concerned I had to temper my natural enthusiasm at our decent start, or as Sam pointed out every time a microphone or journalist were anywhere near him - it was our best start for about eight years, with a couple of nagging doubts that were beginning to surface. Would he continue to find a place for Smith now that everyone was fit? Our midfield was certainly getting stuck in and we all appreciated that but it lacked both creativity and pace meaning the ball would often get bogged down in the middle of the park when we were screaming for Oba or Owen to be released.

Would we always play the big man-little man combo meaning Oba or Owen alongside Viduka or Shola rather than both the little fellas up front together? I would like to have seen us rip into some teams and take a chance occasionally rather than the 'keep it tight' tactic, particularly the lower rated teams like Reading and Derby, we might have won the odd one against them then. Despite my doubts though we had done okay, beating the likes of Wigan, West Ham, Everton and Tottenham. We'd also racked up draws with Boro and the mackems leaving regional pride intact but the defeats we'd suffered had left a feeling that all was not well.

Derby County away was a banker for the three points, they were getting whipped left, right and centre but we lost one- nil and didn't appear to want it enough. Away to Arsenal we didn't expect anything and that's what we got but the scary thing was that we weren't making chances or having shots on target. We visited Man City after that and took the lead through a sublime Martins goal but as soon as they equalised we crumbled, the famed Allardyce 'hard to beat' bubble was bursting.

Our next away game was at Reading where we were comprehensively outplayed and lost again, it's bad enough when it happens at Arsenal but the likes of Reading and Derby rolling us over just made it bloody worrying. When Pompey rolled into town on the third of November I was in Athens as it was my wedding anniversary (cracking town by the way). I enquired at a couple of local bars about English football being on the local telly channels but was met with shrugged shoulders followed by general amusement when I mentioned being a Newcastle fan - it's obviously both a curse and a blessing depending upon where you're from.

When my phone started beeping about eight minutes after kick off I feared the worst, I switched it off eleven minutes after the start and hit the Mythos. Three nil down and out of the game that early is unacceptable no matter what the reason - it was becoming increasingly obvious that something was badly wrong at St. James. We got twatted again in our next home game, Liverpool finishing the game by half time and Sam's abilities and methods were being seriously questioned. I was in the camp that said give him time. He obviously had a blind spot where the likes of Smith and Barton were concerned and had a real aversion to attacking football but, in my opinion, sacking him was the wrong course of action.

The media obviously loved it and stirred up as much discord and negativity as they possibly could before we played Blackburn away, they got what they wanted when we lost again and the game at home to Arsenal on the following Wednesday was being billed as make or break for Big Sam.

The players appeared to have been roused from their slumber for this one and we gained a creditable draw, should arguably even have won, but it begged the question - why hadn't they put that much effort in all season? We had a mini revival at that point beating Birmingham and then Fulham with last minute winners but it was obvious to all that results were masking poor performances and dour football.

I was at the Fulham game (no Richard and Judy this time mind I was very disappointed they stood me up) and it was awful. I have seen some crap games in my time but this was dire. The away fans were as magnificent as ever and gave the team, and the manager, all the backing they could hope for. We were rewarded with a fortunate last minute penalty which was stuck away by Barton (about the only positive contribution he had made up to that point in the season). As an aside to the football someone sadly got stabbed on the tube after our party of five had enjoyed a drunken bounce around London contriving to make us miss our last train home and neccessitating some last minute adjustments to our travel plans - you just can't beat getting off a train in the middle of nowhere at half one in the morning can you?

We then followed this with what surely should have been a certain three points at home to Derby County only to scrape a lucky draw in the eighty seventh minute. They had taken something like eight points all season and four of them were from us - it was shocking to say the least. This preceded three straight defeats and Sam's time was nearly up. No-one but the players and staff know what goes on at the training ground or in the dressing room but the team had quite obviously given up on the manager and, with hindsight, it had happened some time ago. He had one more game in charge, away to Stoke City from the division below, with which to save if not his job then his reputation. We were fortunate to come away from the Britannia Stadium with a no score draw in a boring, midfield battle of a game that characterised Sam's time in charge at Newcastle. I was leaving the very next day for a holiday in America and was looking forward to the delights of Vegas, Los Angeles and San Francisco so wasn't really that bothered assuming we'd do them in Geordieland. My immediate concerns were more travel related as we were getting up at daft o clock for the flight and I still hadn't packed.

It was while we were in the land of the free that news came through of his departure and, while I didn't think it was the right time to be doing it, it had been on the cards for months really. So now the search was on - who would be mental enough to want to manage the toon?

Holidays in the Sun

Whenever something momentous happens in the world people can always remember where they were when they found out the news. You know the kind of thing - Kennedy murdered, the moon landings, England's World Cup win and whenever Beckham gets his hair cut.

Well when Special K came home I was in San Francisco (in a bar surprisingly enough) and having lost contact with the outside world some time ago I was in the dark about our impending appointment. The credit on my phone was completely gone from people texting me about Allardyce's departure and, as you know, the Americans tend not to take much interest in anything outside of their shores - bless em.

So, I'm in this boozer with our lass and there's a football match on the telly at the end of the bar. It can't be? It is - it's Newcastle. She is obviously thrilled by my discovery and continues talking to a couple we've made friends with whilst I strain my eyes trying to work out what match it is.

The shirts are definitely nineties, it's obviously one of those classic match re-runs.

Yeah look, the subtitle at the bottom of the screen says 'Keegan back to Newcastle' we must be playing Man City. Aye that must be it.

Hold on - we're playing Man Utd on there - Keegan never managed them.

Now it's got his managerial career record on screen, they've stopped the match completely. What's gannin on?

I scanned the screen from top to bottom, and the hairs on the back of my neck stood up, goose bumps appeared on my arms and my chest swelled with something I couldn't explain even now.

At the bottom of his record it said simply:-

Newcastle United 2008 - ?

I ordered more beer with a stupid grin on my face, tipped the barman far too much and told everyone who would listen and lots who wouldn't...Keegan was back.

The Second Coming

Wor Kev had swept back into Newcastle on a wave of optimism and goodwill but it couldn't disguise the truth. The ten years between his departure and return had seen a ridiculous amount of money spent on journeymen, average players and mercenaries. The man responsible for that had taken his thirty pieces of silver and gone, he and his sidekicks having made millions off the backs of the support, but had left a club in disarray.

Allardyce had bequeathed a poor Premiership side to Keegan but in truth the roots of the malaise lay with Souness and his spunking of fifty million pounds on utter shite. Big Sam's team had struggled all season but lay in mid-table thanks to a fortunate fixture list that saw us play the less able teams in the division (mind you- we still couldn't beat frigging Derby County) but Kevin had no such luck. He was parachuted in to save us with only two weeks of the transfer window left and he made the brave decision not to waste any money on the few players that might be available - a proper long term view as players are only available in January for one reason, they're shite - a truth we'd discovered to our cost in the past (I still have nightmares about Boumsong).

His first few games saw us play the likes of Villa, Liverpool and Arsenal away (twice). Manchester Utd and Blackburn came to St. James and throw in the fact we had a few local derbies in there with the mackems and the smoggies and you can see he had no easy ride. The national press went for the jugular, they'd made it plain there was some kind of agenda against us anyway but they seemed to really have it in for Keegan and Mike Ashley. The team were low on confidence and as the window had now shut Kev had to work with what he'd got.

Results were disappointing. There'd been talk on the internet message boards of us storming up the table and into the

European places just before we battered Man Utd in the FA Cup final and the chill wind of reality discomfited many.

Me? I knew we'd struggle for the rest of the season. I also knew we wouldn't qualify for any European competition (I'd had my fingers crossed for the fair play league but then twigged that with Smith and Barton in the team maybe that wasn't going to happen) so I didn't get too downhearted. We got tanked in a few games, struggled for both goals and points and relegation was a real possibility but I could look further than the London based tabloid headlines and see the beginnings of a new era at St. James. I went to the Villa game not long after Kev took over and the change in our play was obvious. In the first half we dominated them even though we were carrying the likes of Smith and Barton (slow, and over-rated - that's not me being vicious though Joey - it's just a fucking fact), they couldn't get the ball off us. When Kev had been given enough time to get his own men in then we'd see that start to turn into full games of keeping possession and toying with the better teams.

It was the same in the Blackburn home game a few weeks after that, we destroyed them. Michael Owen could have had a hatrick on his own and Duff, Milner and Smith could also have scored. We let a stupid goal in near the end which was frustrating and meant we'd had another defeat but the team left the park to applause from the majority of fans. The performances were picking up from the Allardyce era, we were attacking again and it was good to watch (well apart from the not scoring and getting beat bit). If you look back at Wor Kev's previous go round at Newcastle he started slowly, he just kept us up in Division two with a mixed bag of results and performances before he got to have a proper pre-season and work with everyone away from the hurly burly of a match every couple of days. Throw into the mix that it also gave him time to plan and execute his transfer policy and it was obvious we should be looking forward to next season with relish.

That summer we stayed up he got rid of half a team and

brought in players of the calibre of Venison, Bracewell, Beresford and (a few weeks later) the mighty Robert Lee. He persuaded them all to sign for a team that was literally minutes from going into Division Three (once again thank you messrs Kelly and Peacock - lest we forget) and then lit the blue touch paper. The parallels that could be drawn between the two seasons were eerily similar: - underperforming players on big money; disenchanted fans; cowardice in the face of the enemy (i.e. good teams!) and, most importantly, a new owner making his first managerial appointment and being prepared to throw buckets of money at making it work (oh how wrong I was about that- but that's in a bit).

So I continued to smile at the social inadequates I worked with as they tried to bait me with jibes about our underachieving club. I dismissed the 'journalists' who would find every excuse possible to have a go at us (you lot could even stop buying their papers - just a thought like) and I ignored the 'pundits' on the telly who repeated gossip, fabrication and rumour as solid fact. My opinion was this:- as Newcastle supporters the best thing we could do was to get behind the lads on the park regardless of whether we thought they deserved to play for us or not. We should make ourselves safe from relegation, write off the season and then book our summer holidays knowing that while we're on the beach and drinking lager for breakfast Kev will be hard at work on our behalf.

He loves the club, he loves us and he's got unfinished business with a few old adversaries. I say it every year but this time I genuinely meant it.

Next season was going to be fucking great.

The Cockney Rejects

Sigh You'd think I'd learn wouldn't you?

The fixture list for '08 - '09 came out and it gave us Man Utd away first game - naturally my first thought was 'Bollocks'. The way I looked at it we could be bottom of the league on goal difference after the first game, the press would have a field day, some of the fans would fall for it and the rest of the season would be a struggle from there on.

Kevin Keegan wouldn't have a bar of it. He declared that he was glad and it was the best time to play them. That was enough for me. If Kevin was confident then so was I and do you know what he was right. We took the game to them, matched their desire with our own and gained a creditable one all draw - in fact they only scored when we were down to ten men. We followed that with a home win against Bolton and our season was off and running. I'd even allowed myself the luxury of looking at the fixture list, predicting results and working out where we'd realistically finish (Champions...if you're asking like).

Then, in true Newcastle fashion, it all came tumbling down around my ears.

Now, in fairness, Mike Ashley did a lot of good stuff when he took over at the toon. Long term season tickets payable in installments, extended family section, consultation with fans, the singing section and even letting flags into games again. Yes, he definitely made some improvements. However, On Thursday 4th September 2008 he wiped out every bit of goodwill he'd built up in one stroke when he chose his friend Dennis Wise over the one man in his whole setup that actually cared about Newcastle United - Kevin Keegan. This allegedly astute businessman managed to lose an entire city of paying customers for all of his businesses in one go.

In truth this had been building for a while. Since Chris

Mort left, the communication emanating from the club had been non-existent but Keegan's body language and general patter weren't right and we'd all started to notice.

He stated unequivocally before the Arsenal away match that 'James Milner is the last person I would like to see leave this club' and a few days later Milner was gone with Kev saying 'It was my decision.' It patently wasn't but Wor Kev seemed upbeat, telling us all 'judge me when the transfer window shuts.' I was happy with that because I knew that Kev meant there was quality players coming in and he'd never let us down before on that score - unfortunately we were all unaware that he wasn't in charge of acquiring them anymore, the buying and selling was down to Dennis Wise.

In hindsight it was blatantly obvious that Keegan had been promised a player better than Milner by the 'recruitment team' (Bastian Schweinsteiger apparently) and come Monday night when the window slammed shut it was also obvious that they'd lied to him. With all due respect to the two players brought in by our elite squad of recruiters (who only ever seemed to go to Spain to sign anyone...) they weren't what the manager wanted. They got him a forward to go with the five we already had and a twenty six year old midfielder who was loaned out to us immediately after signing for his new club - how good was he going to be then?

Unlike the rest of the miscreants that made up the management of Newcastle United Kevin Keegan is a man of principle and honour and there was no way he could allow himself to be used to lie to the fans so Llambias and the cockney posse could pursue their own hidden agenda. Indeed Derek Llambias, ex casino manager and good mate of Mike Ashley (the only qualification needed for a top job at the toon then) was seen at that fateful Arsenal match entertaining David O Leary - one of the then favourites to replace Wor Kev. if I was to suggest there was a conspiracy by the cockney boys to push out Keegan and install their own puppet then that would obviously only be my opinion - it bore thinking about at the time though.

Unfortunately for Dennis Wise (could there be a less apt surname?), Llambias and the other one they made a major mistake if they thought they could patronise us, treat Kevin Keegan with contempt and dismiss the fanbase as insignificant. The entire city was up in arms at the disgraceful treatment of our club and of Keegan and, for once, there were moves afoot to do something about it. There was talk of match boycotts, mass protests and general awkward behaviour not just in and out of St. James but also within Ashley's other businesses. This was designed to hit him where it really hurts his type - in the pocket - and it also put him squarely in the media spotlight a position he apparently didn't relish one bit.

Whilst this was going on I received some good news with regard to my writing. The mighty 'Byker Books' accepted my story 'Blagger' for their inaugaral publication - a collection of short stories about inner city life - and put me on the same pages as the likes of Danny King. The name of the publication - 'Radgepacket' - brilliant eh? The book got a good reception and some people were kind enough to praise 'Blagger' (could easily describe any one in the Newcastle United hierachy that like...) which led me to sending them more stuff - more in hope than expectation I've got to say. They got back to me fairly quickly, asked me to tidy a few bits up and said that they'd be happy to publish 'Rivelino' in summer '09 and would I be amenable to doing a few signings and stuff? Amenable? I had to be physically restrained from running down to the local Waterstone's with me lucky pen there and then!

Luckily we had some beer in the house - that always calms us down.

Then from the sublime to the ridiculous (manager wise anyway) we replaced Keegan with ...Joe Fuckin Kinnear! Now initially I laughed at the sheer desperation of it all but then Joe started to win me over with some battling displays and the fact he kicked off with the national press, who's disdain for our city and club seems very personal for some reason. Following that little surge though we went up and down a bit and Joe's averageness started to shine through. Don't get me wrong, he made us hard to beat (ask Chelsea - HA have that you bunch of whinging, new money, yuppie twats!) and he was a competent enough manager but that was it. If, as was mooted by the 'management' of the club in January, we had kept him on any sort of normal three year contract we could expect to spend those three years in the lower reaches of the league because that is his level - mind you there are some of us who would have been pleased with that as the conclusion to the season approached and we looked doomed.

The January transfer window came and despite promises about strengthening and Fat Mike claiming we would 'drive the club forward together' we sold Shay Given and Charles N' Zogbia before bringing in Kevin Nolan and Ryan Taylor along with the out of contract Peter Lovenkrands. Obviously in true 'spin, spin, spin' fashion there were several last minute bids made for players that we had no chance of getting thus allowing the claim from those running the show (and I use that term very loosely) that they tried and what can you do. They also claimed that they'd 'done everything they could' to keep Given - even though it later transpired that he'd been told he could go three weeks before the end of the window but it wouldn't be announced until the last possible minute in case the fans expected the money to be spent on new players. That told me everything I needed to know about the motives of the owner and his acolytes and the direction they intended on taking Newcastle United.

The club made a profit somewhere in the region of seven Million pounds on the transfers and yet Derek Llambias, the chief stooge of the Ashley reign, made the laughable claim in an interview with the local papers that we were still a 'buying' club. He also claimed that 'the manager has had every player he wanted' - ignoring the fact that the last two incumbents had shouted long and loud about getting a left back and still none was forthcoming from the highly professional recruitment team headed by the poisoned dwarf. It makes you wonder what they'd be like if they weren't listening to the manager and just buying and selling players in order to make a profit for the owner - they'd probably buy spanish forwards that the manager didn't want for half the price they'd just got for selling the best young winger at the club just as he was on the verge of an England call up - lucky that doesn't happen eh?

Oh and did I mention the mackems beat us at their place? In all fairness they were the better team and deserved to win, Richardson's free kick was excellent and frankly after nearly thirty years it had to happen eventually. It seems strange though that their fans can invade the pitch, confront our goalkeeper, make to attack the away supporters and throw bottles and coins at one of our substitutes without a murmur from the FA. I wonder if they would have kept so quiet if it had been a British team in Europe and a load of, say, Turkish fans had behaved that way? I think not.

Actually speaking of Sunderland it was also strange that when Roy Keane left before he was found out after spending another squillion pounds on another two thousand players it didn't cause half the fuss in the press as Keegan leaving did.

Still they'll have all those celebration DVD's, tee-shirts, pictures and key rings of their 'cup final' win against us to sell and raise some more funds to replace what he squandered.

When we played Arsenal at home on March 21st we were in the shit. Just outside of the bottom three by the skin of our teeth (on goal difference) and we needed some points desperately. I was in Berlin, you know me by now, have air miles will travel. Anyway, I knew we'd lose this one, our dream team pairing of Hughton and Calderwood didn't inspire confidence (they don't inspire anyone in fact) and Arsenal had rediscovered their shooting boots. This was gonna be painful.

My most immediate problem was finding somewhere to watch the thing though. I had inadvertently booked a hotel in a gay, red light area of Berlin (fuck off it was an accident man!) and had realised by default. I was about to go into a sports shop to look at some Adidas trainers - I'm a Gazelle's man, proper old school I'm sure you'll agree - when I noticed one of the mannequins wearing a gimp mask. My eyes opened by this discovery I took a proper look around the window display and realised all the models had leather hotpants and caps and stuff on...and they were all blokes. Then I noticed the various clubs and pubs round the place had them little rainbow coloured flags hanging outside the doors and my heart sank. I couldn't not watch the toon but I also couldn't be in a place where men hugged before the team had scored - I'm a good looking boy for fucks sake, who knows what would happen.

Then I saw it, across the main road, a sports bar, no flag hanging outside and still an hour to kick off - cheers God. I headed over and walked in as if I owned the place, the smoke stung my eyes (still allowed over there) and the mainly Turkish clientele regarded me with suspicion...oh and they were all blokes. I ignored them all, I was on Toon business after all, and approached the barman.

'Do you show English football here mate?' I was straight in with the hard talk. No messing.

He looked blank. I pointed at the big screen where a German match was just finishing and tried again.

'English Fussball - Newcastle United?'

He motioned me to wait, I felt like one of them spies in the Cold War and tried to look cool while he walked through the card tables and fruit machines to a settee where he whispered in the ear of what looked like an enormous fat man from the back.

Then it stood up. I was right. He was an enormous fat man. The barman turned and pointed at me whilst Jabba jangled his gold chains amongst his chest hair and looked gangster like. I silently checked out my path to the door, if Jabba the Hood told me to kiss his ring I was offski.

I needn't have worried. He pointed at the screen, nodded, said 'Arsenal' and sat down again. That was me off to get changed.

*****

I headed back into the bar a bit nervously. Having walked past more than one of the gimp mask shops on the way there the word 'Rohypnol' was echoing through my mind and I resolved not to let my drink out of my sight. I sauntered through the door of the bar like I'd drank there all my life and headed to an empty table off to the side and behind the fat gangster's settee. Behind me there was only one empty table - and the bar was a lot less crowded than earlier. So far so good.

I got a beer and settled back to watch the match, the commentary was in German but that wasn't a problem as I could see with my own eyes just how shite we were and didn't need telling. Somehow we got a penalty and Martins stepped up to take it, I braced myself to keep my celebrations to a minimum, I didn't want to draw attention to myself in here. Luckily Martins helped me out by taking one of the worst penalties I've ever seen - thanks Oba, saved my life that like!

We matched them with effort if not skill in the first half and went in at nil-nil. I finished my pint and then risked a piss, no predators in the bogs, belter. Back at the bar my spy training came out again as I ordered a different brand of beer before the second half kicked off in case they'd tampered with the other stuff while I'd been blindsided - as no-one had given me a second glance since I'd entered the bar I may have been a little over-cautious mind.

Taking my seat I noticed that a small band of lads had gathered to play cards right behind me but I didn't have time to worry about that before Arsenal scored. They were celebrating on the screen, my head went down and I knew we were all but relegated. I also noticed the fat gangster making a clenched fist gesture and checking his betting slip - the cheeky bastard had bet against us...wish I had.

From the depths of despair to the height of ecstasy thirteen seconds later when the mighty Arsenal defence conspired to give us a soft goal, well finished by Martins. I wasn't expecting it this time and my five second delay to brace myself against celebrating never had the chance to materialise. I was out of my chair with a primal scream that would have caused an avalanche in the Swiss alps. The gangster and his pals on the settee in front of me visibly flinched before spinning round. The mob of card players behind me jumped up and all eyes were on me.

'Er...sorry.'

'Eet's okay. Heez Eenglish.'

The barman was in to save me - top man. There were nods and smiles all round and I had another pint before Arsenal destroyed us and the fat gangster won his bet.

Whilst waiting for the final whistle I just got to thinking whether the multitude of clowns that have run our club over the years have ever really understood what it means to us and what we go through to be part of it? If you think back to the start of this book you might recall I started following the toon properly in the early Eighties, a time that saw our club selling their star players, the money disappearing and directors that were happy to wallow in mediocrity. Fast forward nearly thirty years and we're right back where we started. I might have changed and grown up but my club hasn't and it's fucking heartbreaking.

The thing is though, the thing that no 'glory boy' or 'armchair expert' will ever understand is this. I can look back over many years of highs and lows. I can remember the players I've seen, the incidents, the goals and the despair. I can remember banter and crack on the terraces with like minded souls that pisses all over the laughs created by professional comedians and I've loved all of it. My club is as much a part of me as my right arm is and if you asked me if I'd change all that to be a supporter of another team, maybe even a team that wins things regularly and has no drama's. An Arsenal or a Man Utd even.

Would I have given it all up to be one of them?

Would I fuck.

Shear Disbelief

On April 1st 2009, with eight games to go until our relegation was confirmed and a growing sense of mutiny on Tyneside, Mike Ashley finally acted. Newcastle's greatest ever goalscorer and Geordie legend Alan Shearer took control of the first team to try and keep us up.

When I heard my first thought was that it was a particularly nasty April Fool's joke, but after it had been confirmed, my second thought was that we'd stay up, storm up the league into the euro places next season and win the FA Cup!

Unfortunately it was not to be and on a lovely sunny Bank Holiday weekend at Villa Park we went down with a whimper. Hull lost at home meaning we only needed a draw to stay up against a team that hadn't won in ages and were already mentally on their holidays but even this was beyond us. Despite a good fifteen minute start when we could have scored twice, a cruel deflection off Damien Duff's boot nestled in the back of our net and that was pretty much it. It was a crap reward for the thousands of us in the away end but it wasn't unexpected. We had played our part and shown defiance in the face of the inevitable, we sang, we chanted, we drank heavily and we supported our team. We are Geordies and this is simply what we do. The pain was kept inside and we behaved like men in front of the many cameras that were willing us to sob like girls.

Afterwards all talk was of awaydays at Blackpool and suchlike, coming back up as champions and destroying every team we faced just like in the early nineties.

In fact, fuck it, I'm getting excited about next season even as I type this...

Jesus wept...here we go again!

Not Nineteen forever

Since I started trying to write back at the start of 2005 I reckon I could have wallpapered my whole house with the rejection slips and letters I've received. My fortunes appear to have mirrored those of the toon as each time I've thought I was getting somewhere the whole lot would come crashing down and I'd have to start again.

But...there is no greater feeling on earth than finishing your first book and the sense of accomplishment that goes with it (if there's any makems looking at this I mean writing it not colouring it in). Having written an article about mine and Col's time at the match and then seeing it published by 'The Mag' (issue 190 if you're interested - not that I'm anal or anything...) I gained in confidence and wrote two fiction novels set in the greatest city on earth. They're currently being bounced around the desks of publishers and agents as we speak (hey - I never said they were any good). My life turned around on the drive home from Geordieland that Christmas, I realised that even a Byker radgy could have a go at following his dream however stupid it might sound to people who perceive you in a certain way.

When it came to telling the world about Col's death it left me a bit stumped. I thought long and hard about how to do it and didn't have a clue really if I'm honest. So in the end I just wrote, as best I could at the time, from the heart, about one of our final matches together. I was reminded of it's existence recently when my nephews persuaded me to have a kickabout outside with them. They think I'm a good player but this is a falsehood that stems from back when they were kids and their mother wanted to watch an England match on the telly. They, instinctively knowing that England were shite even then, didn't want to know until they were told a little white lie (well a fucking big grey one actually).

'But your Uncle Andy plays for England...'

Cue two small family members avidly watching the screen for a balding, overweight, damned handsome Geordie ripping the net asunder with one of his trademark and frequently boasted about rocket shots. Ninety minutes later two disappointed small family members were told that Uncle Andy must have been injured.

Anyway, we're outside in the garden and I'm demonstrating my keepy up skills (I can do four if you want to know...) and teaching them the basics of some essential games - Headers and Volleys, Three pots in, Spot and World Cup. Their footballing masterclass is finished when my sister in law shouts something through the window about this being the last match and I'm immediately back in that place I've often thought about when I'm not quite awake. I can hear the ball banging on the ground and the chatter of kids voices and I know someone will bang on my back door in a minute and ask me mam if Rivs is coming out.

I look at my nephew still half in my daydream and I can see his lips moving but can't quite hear him so I ask him to repeat himself and he says it again.

'I said he's going to be Rooney and I'm going to be Owen, who do you want to be Uncle Andy?'

The birds had halted their singing, there was no traffic hum from the nearby motorway and it was like the very air around me had stopped flowing as everyone and everything craned to hear me say it just once more...

'Me son - I'm Rivelino...'

So, over the page, one last time for my friend Colin Moore from Walker, here is 'The Last Match' - rest in peace mate and remember, when I get up there - it's your round.

See ya.

The Last Match

In the football season 91/92 Newcastle United were rubbish, certain to be relegated to Division 3 and imminent bankruptcy. Kevin Keegan arrived on his white charger and somehow saved us, he followed that miracle by proclaiming he was taking us up to the Premier League in the very next season.

We believed him.

And so, in season 92/93, attendances suddenly shot up to the point of making matches all ticket and locking thousands of fans out of the ground. We all knew why this had happened, Wor Kev had fashioned a team capable of not only promotion but the second division (it will always be division 2, I don't care what Sky TV think) title as well. The fact that he'd done it with a team that came close to being relegated the year before plus a few very good and very reasonably priced additions was a credit to him and his often-criticised management skills and as many thousands of fans who hadn't previously bothered with their local club started to attend St. James it meant that a lot of the lads who'd been there home and away for years were now being locked out.

No more could we get mortal drunk in the Farmers (proper, old school, pre-match boozer) and wobble up to the ground at five to three, we knew in the back of our minds that this was for the good of the club and put up with it. The downside was that it meant that some of the real supporters who'd been there for years and years were turned away never to return - the type of supporter for example who was there when we'd turned a three-nil half time lead into a four-three defeat at home to Charlton the previous year.

After about five games at the start of the season, the football we were playing and the sterility of the newly formed Premier League meant that the tabloids had really started to sit up and take notice of the Toons apparently ceaseless quest to crush everyone in that division and were all running competitions for VIP tickets for various matches.

As we'd been locked out of the Portsmouth and West Ham matches me and my mate Col had entered a few of these in desperation and guess what? We actually won one. The Daily Star sent me two VIP tickets for the home match against Grimsby, this was to be match number twelve of our one hundred percent winning start to the season and for once we could say with certainty we would actually be going.

The week before we had beaten Sunderland at Roker park with 'that' goal by Liam O Brien so Grimsby at home would be a piece of piss, I got a letter through with the tickets saying when to get there and what to wear, no jeans and no football tops. This wasn't really the end of the world as back then (and some of you may find this hard to believe) nobody really wore replica shirts, these were another product of the boom in attendances and the advent of the 'Toon army'.

So on the day we went to our local (the Stags Head in Byker) beforehand and lorded it up a bit in our smart gear, flashed our VIP tickets and exchanged a bit of banter with the lads then headed for the ground. Amazingly, as we still deep down thought it was a hoax, they let us in without any bother and took us to our reception room. Now this was at one o clock a good two hours before kick off (matches used to be played on Saturday at 3pm - strange I know) and the first thing they told us was that all drinks would be free courtesy of the aforementioned paper - smashing.

Bob Moncur then came in to meet us and told us he was our host for the day which was good, he was a nice bloke and answered loads of trivial questions before jokingly telling us that if the lads didn't win today then we were obviously the jinxes, oh how we laughed at the thought of losing at home to Grimsby. We had a couple of pints and then were taken out onto the pitch for our photo to be taken by the newspapers photographer, at this point Sir John Hall came running out asking if anyone could play centre forward as Kev had an injury crisis, even though he was having a laugh I swear every hand went up (mine was first like) sad isn't it.

Back in our room we then had dinner and a couple more pints and then decided to try our luck with a few chasers, to our surprise no one seemed to mind so we had a few more just to be sociable and then a couple more just because we could.

To be honest all I can remember about the match was us two drunkenly shouting and singing for ninety minutes, a bloke called Dobbin scoring a cracker for them near the end and us losing 1-0. Afterwards we were back in the room and had to choose a man of the match, I was having trouble speaking by now so Col did the honours with my vote.

Lee Clark got the award and duly came up to see us, even in the state I was in I could tell he was not happy to have lost and told us they were lucky bastards and not to worry as we would still win the league.

Finally, we were informed we could stay until half past six and then the function rooms would be closing, I just remember us looking at each other and working out how much drinking time we had left...then kicking the arse right out of it!

At about half seven having somehow negotiated getting on and off the bus we wandered back into the Stags Head, greeted with derision by the locals mainly due to the result but probably also because we were absolutely bladdered, however, we won them back over when we emptied our pockets. Packets and packets of cigars acquired from the bar at the expense of the Daily Star were stacked on the table for anyone who wanted them (we'd ate the crisps on the bus), if any coppers had raided the bar that night they'd have thought someone had given birth to sextuplets given the amount of Hamlets being smoked!

That was the last home match me and Col went to together, there were some notable away games that season (Peterborough and Barnsley spring to mind), I managed to dubiously acquire a standing season ticket through a written off car and a gullible insurance company but he couldn't get one. Later that year I moved away down south to look for work and I'm still down here a lot of years later, Col got married and had a kid, we sort of grew up in different directions and didn't see much of each other after that, just bumped into each other every now and then.

I went to his funeral on Christmas Eve, he was gone at the age of thirty five, someone brought up that Grimsby match and the state we were in when we got back to the pub and we all allowed ourselves a smile reminiscing about it.

At the time we didn't know that it was the last one we'd go to together, or even that Newcastle still wouldn't have won anything all these years later but even if we had we'd still have had a good day and supported the team as best we could.

So, If you're reading this at the match and the team are struggling and the atmospheres shite, then bear in mind that you just may not get the chance to be there again and go out of your way to enjoy the experience as much as possible, but above all keep the faith - we did.

Howay the Lads

Rivs